Create The Life You Want Now

Your 90-Day Roadmap to
Purpose, Balance, and Success

I0530490

Marla A. McCarthy

RLS

Real Life Series Publishing

Create the Life You Want Now: Your 90-Day Roadmap to Purpose, Balance, and Success Copyright © 2025 by Marla A. McCarthy

Published by The Real Life Series Publishing Co., LLC. All Rights Reserved.

Available at Amazon.com

No part of this book may be reproduced or transmitted in any form or by any means, electronic or mechanical – including photocopying, recording, or by any information storage and retrieval system – without permission in writing from the publisher. Please direct your inquiries to rlspublishing@gmail.com

First Printing 2025
ISBN: 979-8-9989754-2-4
LCCN: 2025911247

Scripture quotations marked (KJV) are taken from the King James Version of the Bible. All scripture quotations in this book, except those noted otherwise, are taken from the King James Version of the Bible.

Scripture quotations marked (NKJV) are taken from the New King James Version®. Copyright © 1982 by Thomas Nelson. Used by permission. All rights reserved.

Scripture quotations marked (MSG) are taken from The Message. Copyright © 1993, 1994, 1995, 1996, 2000, 2001, 2002. Used by permission of NavPress Publishing Group."

Scripture quotations marked (NIV) are taken from the HOLY BIBLE, NEW INTERNATIONAL VERSION®. Copyright © 1973, 1978, 1984 International Bible Society. Used by permission of Zondervan. All rights reserved. The "NIV" and "New International Version" trademarks are registered in the United States Patent and Trademark Office by International Bible Society. Use of either trademark requires the permission of International Bible Society.

Scripture quotations marked (NLT) are taken from the Holy Bible, New

Living Translation, copyright © 1996, 2004, 2015 by Tyndale House Foundation. Used by permission of Tyndale House Publishers, Inc., Carol Stream, Illinois 60188. All rights reserved.

Scripture quotations marked (AMP) are taken from the Amplified® Bible, Copyright © 1954, 1958, 1962, 1964, 1965, 1987 by The Lockman Foundation, Used by permission." (www.Lockman.org)

Inquiries should be addressed to:
The Real Life Series Publishing Co., LLC.
rlspublishing@gmail.com

DEDICATION

To my husband,

My partner, my friend, my reminder that love is not a feeling but a choice we have to keep making, day after day. This journey hasn't been easy. We've faced situations, pain, loss, trials, and fears that have shaken me to the core, especially the moment I almost lost you to a stroke. That life-altering experience reminded me just how fragile and fleeting this journey together really is.

And yet, here we are. Still standing. Still building. Still believing. Through the hurt, pain, hard lessons, difficult seasons, and healing, through laughter, dreams, and unexpected detours, we have grown. Life hasn't been perfect, but God has got us, and I am so grateful.

Thank you for encouraging my voice, supporting my vision, and helping raise this big, beautiful family together. I'll always treasure the good years, our inside jokes, and the way God continues to restore us through every test life brings.

To our children, my six amazing sons and one beautiful daughter,

You are each my greatest joy, my daily inspiration, and my proudest legacy. Watching you grow into your purpose and pursue your dreams is one of the deepest and most profound honors of my life. I'll never stop cheering for you on the sidelines of your games, competitions, achievements, or in the seats at your performances and graduations, and in every quiet moment you don't even know I'm watching.

Thank you for seeing me, rooting for me, checking on me, praying for me, and for being patient with me as I, too, chase the life I desire. I'm still growing and becoming, and your love and support have meant more than you'll ever know.

This book is for all of us, for the life we're creating together.

With love that runs deep and dreams that still stretch wide,
—*Mom*

TABLE OF CONTENTS

Introduction

Your Life Is Waiting

For I know the plans I have for you," declares the Lord, "plans to prosper you and not to harm you, plans to give you hope and a future. — Jeremiah 29:11, NIV

Have you ever found yourself whispering through tears, "When is it my turn?"

You love deeply, give endlessly, and keep going even when you're running on empty. You're the backbone of your family, the glue holding it all together. Yet somewhere between the packed lunches, late-night laundry, carpool chaos, work demands, desires of friends, and silent prayers, you wonder if there's still room for you in your own life. I get it. I've lived it.

I've spent decades wearing all the hats: wife of over 25 years, mother to seven exceptional children, caretaker, encourager, businesswoman, coach, sister, friend. I've felt the quiet ache of being everything for everyone, while my own dreams sat in the background, waiting patiently for permission to come forward.

I've known the joy of watching my kids thrive, and the heartbreak of losing my mother just weeks after becoming one myself. I've sat at my husband's hospital bedside after his stroke, holding onto faith while navigating fear and uncertainty. I've whispered prayers through clenched teeth and smiled through silent tears.

And through every chapter of joy and heartbreak, one truth anchored me: I still have a life to live, and with God's help, I can reset and create the life I was meant to live.

Why This Book Was Born

In the thick of surviving day to day, and staring down life-or-death moments, I had a sobering realization: if I didn't start carving out space for my dreams, no one else would do it for me. Life forced me to see this clearly: if I kept waiting for permission to pursue my dreams, I'd wait forever. It was on me to make space and fight for what mattered. My dreams couldn't wait for a perfect time. They needed me to make space, now.

That's when this book was born, not from a place of perfection, but from the real-life trenches of motherhood, marriage, moments of chaos, and messy, beautiful growth. It started as a journal to hold me accountable, and it evolved into a life reset system that has been transforming not just my life, but the lives of women just like you.

This isn't just a guide for goal-setting. It's a lifeline. It's a sacred invitation to rediscover who you are, reignite what matters most, and rebuild your life, one faithful, intentional step at a time.

Why Goal-Setting Matters

As women, especially moms, we've been taught to give, serve, and sacrifice. And while that kind of love is powerful, too often we lose ourselves in the process. We forget that our identity isn't found in the roles we play but in the One who created us.

Setting goals isn't selfish; it's sacred. It's how we steward the gifts God placed inside us. It's how we reclaim our identity, renew our strength, and realign our lives with God's plans. When we live with intention, our homes transform, our children take notice, our confidence grows, and our joy becomes contagious.

What You'll Find Inside

This book guides you through a 90-day journey of transformation across all major areas of your life, including faith, physical wellness, finances, relationships, purpose, and more. Each chapter includes relatable stories, practical strategies, biblical wisdom, and grace-filled encouragement to help you rise above life's challenges.

You'll learn how to:

- Shift your mindset from surviving to thriving.
- Set sustainable goals that align with your faith and values.

- Establish daily routines that support your overall well-being.
- Prioritize yourself without guilt.
- Rebuild confidence, clarity, and peace.

This isn't about hustling harder. It's about living wiser. It's about progress, not perfection, one small, powerful, decisive step at a time.

The GRACE Method: Your Life Transformation System

Early in my journey, I found myself longing for a system that was biblical, doable, and gentle. Something that wouldn't overwhelm me, but would still move me forward. That's when the GRACE Method was born.

You'll get the full breakdown of the method in the next section, but here's a quick peek at what's ahead:

G: Ground Yourself in God's Truth: Start each day with the truth about who God says you are.

R: Reflect on Your Current Reality: Pause and take an honest, loving inventory of where you are.

A: Act with Intentional Steps: Take small, meaningful steps that move you forward.

C: Create Consistent Systems: Build habits that stick and support your growth.

E: Embrace Progress Over Perfection: Give yourself grace and celebrate how far you've come.

This method will be your anchor throughout this 90-day life reset. It's simple, powerful, and rooted in biblical truth.

This Book Is For You If...

- You feel like you're constantly pouring out with little left for yourself.
- You long to feel purposeful, peaceful, and present again.
- You've faced burnout, betrayal, or breakdown, and still believe in a comeback.

- You're ready to stop surviving and start living with intention.
- You want practical steps, spiritual strength, and sustainable growth.

Friend, it's not too late. You are not behind. And you are certainly not too broken. That situation or person that you thought broke you, didn't. You're still here.

God's grace is not only sufficient; it's strategic. He's already factored in every detour, delay, and disappointment. What you've walked through isn't wasted. And what lies ahead can be even better than what's behind you.

How to Use This Book

Each chapter includes:

1. Foundational Truths from Scripture
2. Stories from my life and other women like you
3. GRACE-aligned insights for real-life transformation
4. Reflection questions to help you apply the content
5. Actionable steps that are clear and doable
6. Powerful prayers to center you in God's promises

You'll also find space to pause and reflect, access additional resources, and create your own 90-day roadmap, because this isn't just a book; it's a journey.

Let's Do This Together

This is your life reset. Not to become someone else, but to finally become more of who God created you to be. The woman who is grounded in truth, reflects with honesty and hope, acts boldly, creates life-giving habits, and embraces grace every step of the way.

I'm here with you, cheering you on, praying over you, and believing for your breakthrough. It's time, sis. Your bright future is waiting. Let's begin.

With love,
— Marla

The GRACE Method
Your Life Transformation System

My grace is sufficient for you, for my power is made perfect in weakness.
— 2 Corinthians 12:9, NIV

So, you've tried the planners, the checklists, the New Year's resolutions. You've attempted to "get it together" more times than you can count. And while those tools might help for a while, they often leave you feeling more overwhelmed than empowered, especially when life throws curveballs your way.

What you need isn't more pressure to perform. What you need is a system rooted in grace. That's where the GRACE Method comes in, a gentle, powerful system designed for women who are ready to grow without guilt, take action without overwhelm, and walk confidently in the life God has called them to live.

This method isn't about striving harder or adding more to your plate. It's about simplifying your transformation through five grace-filled rhythms that align with God's truth, honor your real-life limitations, and move you forward, one faithful step at a time. Let me walk you through it.

The GRACE Acronym

> G – Ground Yourself in God's Truth
> R – Reflect on Your Current Reality
> A – Act with Intentional Steps
> C – Create Consistent Systems
> E – Embrace Progress Over Perfection

Each letter in GRACE serves as both a mindset and a method, a solid system that guides how you approach your goals, your healing, your home, and your heart.

This isn't a quick fix; it's a way of living with spiritual intention and self-compassion.

G: Ground Yourself in God's Truth

Every transformation begins with truth. Before we set a single goal or make a single plan, we must anchor ourselves in who God says we are, not who the world says, not even who we *feel* we are on our hardest days. When you start here, you start from a position of strength.

Foundation:
- You are loved.
- You are chosen.
- You are equipped and called.
- You are not behind. You are blessed to be able to be still becoming.

Quick Check:
1. What does God say about my identity?
2. How does His love reshape how I view this area?
3. What biblical truth can I cling to today?

Daily Practice:
- Start your day with scripture or a prayer of affirmation.
- Declare: "I am God's beloved daughter."
- Ask yourself: "How can I honor God in this area of my life today?"

R: Reflect on Your Current Reality

Transformation requires honesty with grace. It's time to get real about where you are, not so you can beat yourself up, but so you can begin to rise from your current position. Reflection is about awareness, not shame. It's the moment we pause and say, "This is where I am, and that's okay."

Assessment:
1. What's working in this area of my life?
2. What's not?
3. What patterns do I see?
4. Where do I feel stuck?

Quick Check:
1. Where do I rate on a scale of 1–10?
2. What has helped me move forward in the past?
3. What's my biggest challenge here?

Weekly Practice:
- Journal without judgment.
- Track patterns and triggers.
- Celebrate every bit of progress, yes, even the baby steps.

A: Act with Intentional Steps

Small steps. Steady progress. Real results. You don't need a 50-point plan. You don't need perfection. You need the *one* next right step, something small enough to do but significant enough to matter. This is about choosing movement over stagnation and intentionality over burnout.

Action:
1. What is one small step I can take today to make a positive change?
2. What feels doable rather than daunting?
3. How can I set myself up to succeed?

Implementation:
- Pick 1–3 small, specific actions in each area.
- Keep commitments short (5–10 minutes to start).
- Focus on building momentum through consistency.

C: Create Consistent Systems

Routines are the rails your goals run on. Systems aren't there to box you in; they're there to hold you up. Think of them as the quiet framework of your daily life: the habits and rhythms that make grace easier to live out and growth feel less like a grind. They are structures that make thriving sustainable rather than exhausting. The right systems don't drain you, they free you.

Structure:
1. What would make this easier to do every day?
2. Where can I build this into what I'm already doing?
3. What support or tools would help?

System Building:
- Use "habit stacking" (After I __, I will __).
- Set visual cues and gentle reminders.
- Build in loving accountability: faith-filled friends, checklists, apps.

E: Embrace Progress Over Perfection

Let's throw out the guilt and celebrate grace. You are not a project. You are a person loved deeply by God and growing day by day. Perfection is not the goal. Progress is. Faithfulness is. Growth, even slow, even messy, is still progress.

Grace:
1. How can I show myself grace today?
2. What progress have I made, even if it's small?
3. What would I tell my best friend in this situation?

Mindset:
- Celebrate your wins, even the ones that may be invisible.
- Learn from what didn't work, without self-blame.
- Remember: God's love isn't earned by performance.

The GRACE Method in Real Life

You'll use this method throughout the 90-day journey as your personal compass and check-in tool. Whether you're tackling finances, fitness, relationships, or rest, GRACE becomes the lens that keeps your heart soft, your steps steady, and your progress sustainable.

Here's what it looks like in action:
- A 5-minute daily GRACE check to center your heart and direction
- A 15-minute weekly review to celebrate growth and adjust gently

- A 30-minute monthly reset to re-align, refine, and re-energize

You'll also learn how to apply GRACE to several critical life areas like:

1. Physical Health: From burnout to energy with grace and intention
2. Financial Health: Stewarding resources with wisdom and peace
3. Organization: Creating a peaceful, life-giving environment
4. Relationships: Loving others while honoring your own needs
5. Purpose/Career: Pursuing your God-given calling without guilt
6. Personal Growth: Becoming who God created you to be, inside and out
7. Joy/Recreation: Embracing rest, fun, and celebration

We'll go through these in detail, step by step. There's no rush. No pressure. Just grace and progress.

You're Not Too Late, You're Right on Time

Sweet sister, you may feel like you've fallen behind in life. Maybe you've lost your joy. Perhaps you feel stuck, uncertain, or tired. But hear me clearly:

- You are not behind. You are building.
- You are not broken. You are being rebuilt into a stronger version of you.
- You are not forgotten. You are God's beloved.
- You don't need more time. You need more **faith** concerning what you can still accomplish with the time you have.

With the GRACE Method, you don't have to hustle for healing or fight your way to fulfillment. You get to walk with God with clarity, courage, and compassion for yourself. And day by day, step by step, you will create the life He's calling you to. Let's get started, together. God's grace has already gone before you.

Therefore, if anyone is in Christ, the new creation has come: The old has gone, the new is here! - 2 Corinthians 5:17, NIV

CHAPTER 1

The Power of Intentional Living

Discovering Your Divine Design

She is clothed with strength and dignity; she can laugh at the days to come.
— Proverbs 31:25, NIV

You can't create the life you want by accident. You have to do it on purpose with prayer, with power, and with a plan.

Maybe you've started a new goal before. You bought the pretty planner. Lit the candle. Made the Pinterest board. You felt inspired and said to yourself, "This is my season." But then life happened. A child got sick. Work exploded. Someone needed you again. And little by little, your dreams faded into the background behind the chaos. Sound familiar?

Sis, hear me clearly: you're not lazy, and you're not failing. You've simply been trying to create a meaningful life without the clarity, support, and strategy you deserve. This chapter is where that ends.

Where Are You Now? A Quick Self-Check

Before we go any further, let's pause and check in. This isn't a test; it's a mirror. Answer honestly and gently. Rate each of the following from 1–5 (1 = Never, 5 = Always):

- ☐ I wake up excited about my day.
- ☐ I know what my priorities are and stick to them.
- ☐ I feel confident in my ability to achieve my goals.
- ☐ I have a clear vision for my future.
- ☐ I make time for things that matter to me.
- ☐ I feel connected to my purpose.

☐ I handle setbacks without giving up entirely.
☐ I celebrate my progress, not just perfection.

Your Score:
32–40: You're already living intentionally! Let's level up.
24–31: You're on the right track, time to fine-tune.
16–23: You're ready for significant, positive change.
8–15: You're right where you need to be to start fresh.

The Problem with "Accidental Living"

Let me introduce you to Sarah, a 34-year-old wife, mom of two, and successful marketing director. On paper, her life looked perfect. But one night, sitting alone in her parked car after a 12-hour day, she realized something gut-wrenching: She didn't feel present in her own life.

"I kept waiting for someday," she told me. "When the kids were older. When work slowed down, when I had more time, but it never came. I realized I was disappearing in my own story."

Sarah's story is heartbreaking, but it's not uncommon. So many women are unintentionally living on autopilot. They're surviving, not thriving. They're stuck in reactive mode, not realizing they have the power to choose a different path.

The Science Behind Living on Purpose

Research conducted by Dr. Gail Matthews at Dominican University found that individuals who write down their goals are 42% more likely to achieve them. When combined with accountability and progress tracking, success rates skyrocket to over 70%.

But this isn't just about goal-setting. Positive psychology shows that intentional living leads to:

- 23% lower levels of cortisol (stress hormone)
- 40% higher life satisfaction
- Longer, healthier lives
- Better relationships and stronger marriages

The research confirms what God's Word has already promised: when we live on purpose, with purpose, we flourish.

Rediscovering Your "Why"

Most women don't lose momentum because they lack the capability. They lose momentum because they get busy and lose connection to why they started. Your *why* is your fuel. It's the heartbeat of your goal. It's what steadies you when life gets messy, when the dishes pile up, the baby's crying, the car breaks down, or someone questions your worth. Let's say your goal is to get in shape. The real why might be:

- "I want to feel strong in my own body again."
- "I want to play with my kids without getting winded."
- "I want my daughter to see a woman who takes care of herself."

That's deeper than just pounds lost or jeans zipped, it's about legacy, confidence, freedom.

My Why (And Why It Keeps Me Going)

There were many seasons of my own life that I felt invisible, buried under laundry, late-night feedings, carpool lines, home life, marriage, parenting, and business stress. There were nights I cried on the bathroom floor, whispering, *"God, what am I doing all this for?"* And He always brought me back to this:

- Because I want my daughter to know she's worthy, seen, and powerful.
- Because I want my sons to know that strong women love deeply and live boldly.
- Because I want other women to know they don't have to choose between motherhood and meaning.
- Because I want to honor the woman God created me to be, not just the roles I play.

Coaching Truth: The 1% Rule

James Clear, author of *Atomic Habits*, says that if you achieve just a 1% improvement every day, the growth compounds into something unstoppable.

Change doesn't live in big, dramatic moments. It lives in:

- A 10-minute walk between errands
- Choosing water over soda
- Saying something kind to your husband when you're tired
- Encouraging yourself in the mirror when your hair is a mess and yesterday's leggings are still on

Think of your goals like seeds. You wouldn't dig them up just because they didn't bloom overnight. You give them time. You nurture them, water them, and let God do the growing.

When My Life Fell Apart

When my husband suffered from multiple strokes, life as I knew it shattered. One moment I was preparing everything for Christmas which was a day away, while trying to keep up with the kids' sports and activities.

The next, I was suddenly back and forth to the hospital for weeks, managing my husband's care, holding up our home, parenting seven children, and trying not to fall apart.

I had every excuse to press pause on my dreams, or lose hope of a future at all. But I didn't. Because I knew that if I didn't do something, anything, for me in the midst of all this chaos, I would lose myself.

So I walked. I prayed. I stretched. I drank water. I breathed. I looked in the mirror and said, "Marla, you're doing better than you think."

That was my beginning. Strength came slowly. But it came. And no matter what you are currently facing, it will come for you too.

Battle the Voice of Self-Doubt

Sometimes the enemy isn't "out there." It's the inner voice saying:

- "You're too tired."
- "You've tried before and failed."
- "Who do you think you are?"
- "You don't have what it takes."

Let's rewrite those lies.

Exercise:
1. Write down one goal.
2. Write every reason you think you can't do it.
3. Now flip every single one into a truth-filled declaration.

Example:
- "I'm not consistent." to "I am becoming more disciplined each day."
- "I never follow through." to "I'm learning to keep promises to myself."
- "It's too late for me." to "God's timing is perfect. He's just getting started."

Intentional Living: A God-Honoring Choice

Some women wonder if it's selfish to pursue goals amid other responsibilities and people relying on them. Let me lovingly say, it's not. God delights in women who steward their gifts well.

Think of Esther, Priscilla, the Proverbs 31 woman; they each pursued purpose, managed their homes and businesses, and shaped history. So can you.

Intentional living rests on **three biblical foundations:**

1. Clarity: Knowing what you want and why
2. Consistency: Taking action in alignment with your values
3. Community: Surrounding yourself with support and accountability

Applying the GRACE Method

As you begin living with intention, the GRACE Method will be your steady compass.

☐ G: **Ground yourself** each morning in God's truth; remind yourself that you are chosen and capable.

☐ R: **Reflect honestly** on where you are right now and what has kept you from showing up for your dreams.

☐ A: **Act by taking one small, purposeful step** today toward the vision God has placed in your heart.

☐ C: **Create consistent systems** by building a simple routine to revisit your "why" daily, whether it's through journaling, prayer, or quiet time. And above all,

☐ E: **Embrace progress over perfection.** You don't need to have it all figured out to start. You just need to begin with grace, faith, and the belief that your transformation is already in motion.

Action Steps for This Week

☐ Complete the *Personal Vision Exercise* (see the end of this chapter)
☐ Identify three life areas you want to transform.
☐ Find an accountability partner or join our online community to support your goals.
☐ Begin your morning with this question: "How can I live intentionally today?"

Reflection Questions:

1. What's one area of your life that feels "accidental" instead of intentional?
2. What goal matters most to you right now?
3. What's your "why" behind the goal that matters most right now?
4. What lie have you believed about yourself that needs to be rewritten with God's truth?
5. What's one small, faith-filled step you can take today?

Prayer of Intention

Heavenly Father,

Thank You for the breath in my lungs and the purpose in my heart. I know You've created me for more than just survival. Help me to live with intention, grace, and courage. Give me vision for the life You designed and the strength to step into it, even when it feels hard. Quiet every lie, every fear, and every voice that tells me I'm not enough. Today, I choose to believe that I am becoming who You made me to be.

In Jesus' name, amen.

Chapter 1 Summary

Key Takeaways:

- Intentional living is a spiritual decision; it honors your divine design.
- Your "why" is the foundation of lasting motivation.
- Tiny steps lead to lasting change.
- You are not selfish for dreaming; you are faithful for pursuing your purpose.

This Week's Focus:

Rediscover your "why," name your vision, and take one bold, beautiful step toward the life God is calling you to live.

PERSONAL VISION EXERCISE

Create the Life You Want Now: On Purpose

Write the vision and make it plain on tablets, that he may run who reads it.
— Habakkuk 2:2, NKJV

Take time to sit in a quiet space with your journal, notebook, or the pages at the back of this book. Pray before you begin, asking the Holy Spirit to guide your thoughts and actions. These questions aren't about getting the "right" answers; they're about getting honest, bold, and spiritually aligned.

1. Your Current Reality

- What does your life feel like right now, in one word?
- What areas feel out of balance, neglected, or draining?
- What are you tolerating that God never asked you to carry?
- Where are you thriving right now?

2. Your God-given Dreams

- If fear, guilt, or shame weren't a factor, what would you pursue?
- What dream keeps coming back to your heart no matter how many times you push it aside?
- What does the God-designed version of your life look like?

3. Your Why

- Why do you want to change your life right now?
- Who will benefit if you grow, heal, and succeed?
- What is the cost of staying stuck?
- What would it mean for you to feel proud of yourself again?

4. Your Identity in Christ

- What lie about yourself are you ready to release today?
- What truth does God speak over your life instead?
- How would you live differently if you truly believed that you are already equipped, chosen, and worthy?

5. Your Next Step

- What is one small, intentional action you can take this week to move toward your vision?
- Who can encourage or support you on this journey?
- What daily habit would keep you focused and aligned?

Optional Prompt for Your Journal:

"The woman I am becoming is…"

Write a full paragraph or letter to yourself describing the strong, confident, faith-filled woman you are becoming in this next season. Speak life over her.

CHAPTER 2

The Framework for Goal Setting

Creating Goals That Actually Work: The SMARTER Framework for Faith-Filled Women

Write the vision, and make it plain... — Habakkuk 2:2, KJV

You've taken the first bold step toward intentional living by identifying your "why." Now, let's build on that clarity with a plan that works in your real, beautifully chaotic life. Not a rigid, color-coded planner fantasy, but a grace-filled system that fits into your everyday rhythm as a woman, a mother, a wife, a professional, or all of the above.

Because here's the truth: dreams without a plan are just pretty wishes. But when you combine your vision with faith and structure? That's where breakthrough begins.

Why Traditional Goal Setting Often Fails Women

You've heard the typical goals before:

- "I'm going to lose 30 pounds this year."
- "I'll finally read my Bible more."
- "I'll start that business... someday."

Sound familiar?

The problem isn't in your desire; it's in the method. Most goal-setting advice was designed for people with uninterrupted time, minimal emotional load, and zero toddlers. In other words, not women juggling homes, emotions, careers, marriages, relationships, community impact, and spiritual growth. We need a better way. A grace-based, faith-rooted, life-friendly way.

Why the 90-Day Reset Works

Here's why 90 days is your sweet spot:
- It's short enough to maintain focus
- Long enough to see real change
- Matches natural rhythms: school semesters, seasons, business quarters, spiritual cycles

This timeline helps you stay energized without getting overwhelmed. And you'll learn to reset and start fresh every 90 days, because life changes, and so can your goals.

Meet the SMARTER Framework

You may have heard of the traditional SMART goals framework (Specific, Measurable, Achievable, Relevant, Time-bound). But I teach something better, something a little smarter.

Why? Because your goals should not only be strategic, but recorded and real…They should light you up.

Here's what **SMARTER** stands for:

S – Specific: Clearly defined. Vague goals = vague results.

M – Measurable: Know how you'll track progress.

A – Achievable: Set yourself up to win. Start where you are.

R – Relevant: Aligns with your values and your current season.

T – Time-bound: Set a clear deadline, like, say, 90 days.

E – Exciting: It should move you. If it feels like a chore, revise it.

R – Recorded: Don't just think it; write it down. That's when it becomes real, and becomes a future record of all that you have accomplished and all that God has done in your life.

"A goal in your head is a wish. A goal in writing is a plan."

From Vague to Vibrant: Goal-Setting Examples

Not This: "I want to be healthier."
Try This: "I will walk 30 minutes, 5 days a week for 90 days to boost energy, lower my blood pressure, and feel stronger."

Not This: "I want to grow spiritually."
Try This: "I will spend 15 minutes reading one chapter of the Bible each morning and journaling my reflections."

Do you feel the difference? One is foggy. The other has feet.

The Power of One: Focus for Maximum Impact

Here's the truth: You can do anything, but not everything at once.
For the next 90 days, choose:

- 1 Primary Goal (your main focus, gets 60% of your energy)
- 1–2 Supporting Goals (smaller goals that enhance the primary one)

This focused approach helps you move forward without burnout. And guess what? The momentum you build in one area spills over into others.

Vision Boards with Intention

I'm a mother of seven, and still have a youthful heart and spirit. So yes, I still love glue sticks and glitter, but this isn't just crafting. It's a spiritual practice. God gave Abraham stars and Joseph dreams. Visualization is biblical.

Steps to Create a Faith-Filled Vision Board:

1. Start with prayer. Ask the Holy Spirit to give you a glimpse of where He's taking you.
2. Focus on feelings. How do you want to feel: peaceful, strong, free?
3. Select 3–5 images max to reflect that.

4. Include action photos (not just the outcome, but the process).
5. Add scriptures, affirmations, and declarations.
6. Display it. Place it where your spirit can see it every day.
7. Update it as you grow. Your vision will evolve, and that's beautiful.

Journaling With God: Your Secret Weapon

Your journal isn't just a planner; it's your sanctuary. It's where you meet with God, sort your emotions, declare your desires, and track His faithfulness.

Try journaling with prompts like:

- "What am I grateful for today?"
- "What progress did I make?"
- "What held me back?"
- "What is God saying to me right now?"
- "What do I need to surrender?"

Some of your biggest breakthroughs won't happen on the stage; they'll happen in private, on a page.

Real Story: Jessica's 47 Goals

Jessica came to me with a list of forty-seven goals. She was tired, discouraged, and stuck in a cycle of "trying everything" and succeeding at nothing.

We narrowed her list to 1 primary and 2 supporting goals. She began to feel focused, energized, and empowered. Within 90 days, she had lost weight, decluttered her home, and reconnected with her children in meaningful ways.

She didn't need more willpower; she needed a strategy and to take one small step today. Now she uses the SMARTER method every season, and she's thriving.

Common Mistakes (And Grace-Filled Fixes)
1. **All-or-Nothing Thinking:** Choose grace and adjust the goal, not

your worth.

2. **Setting Goals for the Wrong Season:** Honor where you are. A mom of toddlers has different bandwidth than an empty-nester, and that's okay.

3. **Quitting After One Missed Day:** Plan for setbacks. Build grace into the system.

SMARTER Goal Worksheet

You can use template or recreate it in your journal:

Primary Goal:
1. What: _____
2. Ultimate Why: _____
3. Success Looks Like: _____
4. Deadline: _____
5. Weekly Action Steps: _____
6. Daily Habits: _____
7. Progress Tracker: _____

Supporting Goal(s):
1. What: _____
2. How it Supports My Main Goal: _____
3. Actions: _____

Action Steps for This Week:

☐ Choose 1–3 SMARTER goals
☐ Complete the worksheet (or journal it)
☐ Create your vision board.
☐ Schedule your first weekly reset check-in.
☐ Share your goals with your accountability partner.
☐ Clear your calendar of distractions for Week 1

Applying the GRACE Method
As you embark on intentional goal-setting, utilize the GRACE Method

to guide your mindset and momentum.

☐ G: **Ground yourself in the truth** that God placed these desires in your heart.

☐ R: **Reflect honestly** on what's realistic and relevant in this season.

☐ A: **Act** by writing out your SMARTER goals and taking one small step today.

☐ C: **Create consistent systems** by choosing your weekly reset time and starting your journaling habit. And most of all,

☐ E: **Embrace progress over perfection.** You don't have to do everything right; you just have to keep showing up with faith and grace.

Reflection Questions

1. What's one vague goal you've held onto that you can now rewrite using the SMARTER method?
2. How do you want to feel at the end of these 90 days?
3. What part of your vision excites you most, and why?
4. What systems or habits can you begin this week to support your growth?

Prayer of Focus & Faith

Father God,

Thank You for giving me vision and the ability to dream. Today, I surrender every scattered goal and invite You to help me focus on what matters most. Show me what to pursue in this season, and give me the wisdom to build goals that honor You and care for my soul.

Help me be faithful in the small steps, and full of grace when I fall short and miss the mark. May every goal reflect Your goodness and bring glory to Your name.

In Jesus' name, amen.

Chapter 2 Summary

Key Takeaways:
• Traditional goals don't work for women juggling real life, SMART-

ER ones do.

- Limit your focus to 1–3 goals to avoid burnout.
- Create a vision board as a faith-filled visual anchor.
- Make space for what sets your soul on fire, regularly.
- Prioritize what fuels your passion and brings you joy.
- Journaling this journey helps you hear from God and track your transformation.
- Grace is the secret ingredient to sustainable success.

This Week's Focus:

Do more of what makes you come alive, and keep something in your week that makes you feel like you again. Define SMARTER goals, build systems, and start walking boldly toward the life God has called you to create.

CHAPTER 3

Daily Routines for Success

Creating Winning Systems: Daily Rhythms That Restore, Not Deplete

She gets up while it is still night; she provides food for her family...
— Proverbs 31:15, NIV

Let's begin with a truth I wish someone had whispered to me years ago: You were never meant to live your life in chaos. You were created for peace, not pressure. For purpose, not panic. And friend, your days don't run you. You run your days.

We often think success shows up in the big moments: launching a business, finishing that degree, paying off the debt, or finally hitting our health goals. But real transformation? It's built in the hidden, sacred, disciplined spaces of our daily routines.

It's in how we start our mornings, how we quiet our evenings, and how we choose to show up in the messy middle. Especially for women and mothers carrying the weight of the world on their shoulders, routines are not just helpful; they are essential.

They're precious and holy. They are anchors of sanity in seasons of storm.

So in this chapter, you're getting a permission slip to release the Pinterest-perfect pressure and embrace a system that works for you. Habits that reflect your season, structure that supports your soul, one that helps you move forward with purpose, without falling apart.

The Myth of the Perfect Routine

Let's bust a myth right now: No one wakes up every day with a flawless routine where everything goes right all the time. If someone says they do, they're either fibbing or not raising small children or teenagers. What does work is a grace-based system, one that's flexible, consistent, and grounded in God's truth. Success isn't about getting it perfect. It's about showing up with intention, again and again. It's about being thankful you get to show up, again and again, especially when life gets messy.

My Morning Routine: Real, Messy, and Sacred

There were seasons I woke up already behind: to burnt waffles, missing shoes, forgotten homework, a toddler crying for juice, and my own heart completely depleted before the sun even rose. I lived on defense.

Eventually, I said, enough. Not in a dramatic overhaul. Just in a tiny, grace-filled decision: "I'm going to reclaim my mornings, one breath at a time."

Here's what my mornings look like now, not perfect, but powerful:

- Opening my eyes with a "thank You, God" in my spirit and on my lips. I try to remember not to get started without a "Holy Spirit, have Your way" in my heart and spoken out of my mouth. Because inviting God's divine intelligence sets the tone for my whole day.
- Time with God: 10–15 minutes in prayer, scripture, a sermon, or worship music. It centers me before the chaos begins.
- Gentle movement & hydration: A glass of water before coffee, a few stretches, and a reminder that my body is God's temple.
- Gratitude & goals: I jot down 3 things I'm thankful for and my top 3 priorities for the day. As often as I can, I write in my prayer journal as well.
- Warming up the environment in the house: I try to set the emotional tone with a kind word, a hug, or a smile, even if I'm still in my robe or pajamas.

Not every day goes smoothly. But I no longer start from empty. I start from anchored. You don't have to do it my way, but you do have to reclaim your mornings because no one will do it for you.

Evening Rituals: Winding Down with Grace

Evening rituals and routines are critical too. They're your reset button. Your moment to exhale, reflect, and reconnect with God in you (Colossians 1:27).

Here's how I protect my peace at night:

- Evening prayer check-in: "God, where did I see You today? Where do I need to grow?"
- Journal reflections: I write down 3 wins, 1 lesson learned, and 1 thing I'm surrendering to God.
- Connection moments: I do my best to engage with my children and spend quality time with my husband. Even 3-5 minutes of laughter, hugs, or prayer can keep us rooted.
- Screen-free wind-down: I turn off devices after 9 p.m. to let my brain and spirit recharge.

These rituals don't require hours; they just require intention.

The Power of Micro-Routines and Grace Habits

Real life happens. Kids get sick. Work gets wild. Hormones get hormonal. Motivation disappears. That's why discipline must be gentler and built for real life.

Try this: **"Remind Me Why I Started" Wall:**

Create a special, sacred space on your wall, mirror, or planner with:

- A photo of your loved ones
- A life-giving verse or quote
- A note to your future self

Speak it out loud when you want to quit. And remember:

And let us not grow weary while doing good, for in due season we shall reap if we do not lose heart. — *Galatians 6:9, NKJV*

"Three Before Ten" Challenge

Before 10 a.m., do these 3 simple things for YOU:
- ☐ Drink water.
- ☐ Read or pray one scripture.
- ☐ Move your body for 5–10 minutes.

These micro-moments ground you without guilt.

Self-Care Is Not Selfish, It's Smart

Let's redefine self-care. It's not selfish. It's smart. It's stewardship. It's not about spa days (though those are lovely if and when you can). It's about restoration before burnout. It's about being well enough to keep becoming who God created you to be.

What Self-Care Looks Like:

- Taking a 15-minute reset with tea and a Psalm
- Pausing for a midday Bible app check-in
- Asking for help instead of pretending you're fine
- Scheduling joy, yes, joy! Like it's a meeting
- Wearing something that makes you feel radiant, even at home

If you haven't been caring for your whole self (mind, body, and spirit), it's time to start. Not tomorrow. Not when things calm down. Not when everyone else's needs are finally met. Today.

Because you, dear sis, are not just a helper. You are a vessel of purpose, a daughter of the King, and a carrier of divine destiny. In order to fulfill the beautiful plans God has for your life, you must be strong enough to stand, wise enough to discern, healthy enough to endure, and spiritually grounded enough to lead with love and grace.

Your well-being isn't a luxury; it's a divine responsibility. Your body is not an afterthought. Your mind is not a battlefield to ignore. Your soul is not meant to be poured out endlessly without ever being filled.

Scripture reminds us:

Do you not know that your body is a temple of the Holy Spirit who is within you, whom you have received as a gift from God...?— *1 Corinthians 6:19, AMP*

You are holy ground and sacred space. It's time to treat yourself like it. So begin to nourish yourself, not from a place of guilt, but from a place of reverence. Eat foods that give you energy. Move your body in ways that honor your strength. Feed your mind with truth, not fear. Speak life over yourself, even when it feels awkward. And protect your spirit with prayer, praise, and God's Word.

You only get one body. One mind. One life. And there is a calling over yours that is too important to neglect. Let today be the turning point. The moment you say, "I am worth caring for, because I belong to God."

My Breaking Point (and My Breakthrough)

There was a day when it all hit at once: sports, school, spilled juice, ten baskets of laundry, and no clean forks left in the house. I locked myself in the closet, slumped to the floor, and cried in silence like I hadn't in years. And in that silent space, God whispered,

"Daughter, I never asked you to do it all. I asked you to abide in Me."

That moment changed my life. I realized, when I'm *that* upset, I'm not abiding in Him. I've taken my eyes off Him. I also realized that rest is not a reward. Self-care is not selfish. I am not the Savior; Jesus is. And I can't control people, they are only changed or transformed on "God's Potter's Wheel". It's not my job.

In these moments when I break down, it's time to pray, invite God's presence and power into the situation, rest, and then take my next step.

Yet, O Lord, You are our Father; We are the clay, and You our Potter,
And we all are the work of Your hand. — Isaiah 64:8, AMP

I have permission from God to look away from the situation, to look up, pray, and then peacefully rest.

Real-Life Self-Care Practices That Actually Work:

Have daily and weekly self-care habits and routines:

- ☐ Light a candle and journal a scripture: Engages your senses and spirit.
- ☐ Solo grocery run with worship music: Combines peace and productivity.
- ☐ Dress in something that makes you feel beautiful: Restores identity.
- ☐ Schedule a "Mama" or "Me" Hour" where no one asks you anything: Rebuilds your boundaries.
- ☐ Go for a prayer walk: Moves your body and lifts your soul.

Coaching Check-In:

1. How am I really doing today?
2. What can I let go of right now?
3. Am I running on God's grace, or just fumes?

God's Word for Your Weary Heart

Reflect and meditate regularly on the following Scriptures:

He makes me to lie down in green pastures; He leads me beside the still waters. He restores my soul; He leads me in the paths of righteousness For His name's sake.
— Psalm 23:2-3, NKJV.

In returning and rest you shall be saved; In quietness and confidence shall be your strength. — Isaiah 30:15, NKJV.

Be still, and know that I am God; I will be exalted among the nations, I will be exalted in the earth! — Psalm 46:10, NKJV.

Come to Me, all you who labor and are heavy laden, and I will give you rest.
— Matthew 11:28, NKJV.

Final Thoughts: Your Routines and Rhythms Reflect Your Worth

Sweet sister, you are not a machine. You are not just a helper or a doer. You are a daughter of the King, worthy of rest, joy, peace, and purpose. Your routines don't have to look like anyone else's. They just need to work for your real life, in your real season, supported by real grace.

Start with one step. One prayer. One breath. And build from there. You're doing better than you think. And I'm here, cheering you on every step of the way.

Applying the GRACE Method

Use the **GRACE** Method to build rhythms that nourish instead of deplete.

☐ G: **Ground yourself** in the truth that your worth is not tied to

performance.
- ☐ R: **Reflect** on where your days feel most chaotic or draining.
- ☐ A: **Act** by adding one small soul-restoring habit this week.
- ☐ C: **Create systems** by stacking simple routines into your mornings or evenings.
- ☐ E: **Embrace progress over perfection** because this journey isn't about doing it all. It's about doing what matters most with grace.

Reflection Questions

1. Which part of your daily routine feels the most chaotic, and why?
2. What would a grace-filled, God-honoring rhythm look like in your mornings or evenings?
3. How can you redefine self-care in your current season?
4. What is one thing you could remove or simplify to make room for rest?

Prayer of Rhythm and Restoration

Lord,

Thank You for designing me with love. Help me create rhythms that restore, not exhaust me. Show me how to protect my mornings, rest in my evenings, and show up in my days with grace, God-given strategy, and clarity. Teach me to pause, to breathe, and to abide in You. Help me let go of guilt and embrace rest as a holy practice. In the places I've been running on empty, pour out Your strength and peace.

In Jesus' name, amen.

Chapter 3 Summary

Key Takeaways:
- Daily routines are not about perfection; they're about peace.
- Morning and evening rituals help you feel anchored, not overwhelmed.
- Self-care is stewardship of your God-designed body, mind, and soul.
- Rest is holy, and joy is spiritual. It comes from God (Genesis 2:2 , Genesis 2:3, Exodus 20:11, Matthew 11:28, Nehemiah 8:10).

Small, intentional habits and systems will take you further than enormous, chaotic efforts. And rest and reconnecting with God are critical.

Come to Me, all you who labor and are heavy laden, and I will give you rest.
—*Matthew 11:28, NKJV*

Do not sorrow, for the joy of the Lord is your strength.—*Nehemiah 8:10, NKJV*

This Week's Focus:

Design one grace-filled routine that fits your life and restores your soul, then commit to practicing it, one day at a time.

GRACE-BASED DAILY RHYTHM AND HABIT TOOLKIT

1. Self-Care Checklist (Realistic & Restorative)

☐ Light a candle and journal a scripture
☐ Take a solo grocery run while listening to worship music
☐ Wear something that makes you feel beautiful, even at home
☐ Schedule a weekly 'Mama or Me Hour', uninterrupted time for YOU
☐ Take a 10-minute prayer walk around your neighborhood
☐ Read one Psalm while sipping tea (no screens allowed)
☐ Ask for help, with no guilt attached
☐ Re-watch a favorite uplifting movie or comedy
☐ Call or text a life-giving friend just to reconnect
☐ Do one small thing today that brings you joy

2. Micro-Routines That Actually Work

Morning Anchor (10–15 mins)

☐ Read or listen to a devotional
☐ Drink a full glass of water
☐ Do 2–3 minutes of gentle stretching
☐ Set 3 priorities for your day
☐ Speak one affirmation out loud

Midday Reset (5–10 mins)

- ☐ Step outside and take three deep breaths
- ☐ Pray or listen to worship music
- ☐ Reflect: 'What do I need right now?'

Evening Wind-Down (15–20 mins)

- ☐ Tidy your space for 5–10 mins
- ☐ Write three wins, one lesson, one prayer
- ☐ Disconnect from screens
- ☐ Read one scripture before bed

3. Weekly Routine Builder

- ☐ Identify your peak energy time (when you feel most focused)
- ☐ Choose your three must-do goals for the week
- ☐ Choose 1 morning and 1 evening routine to implement
- ☐ Set a Weekly Planning Power Hour time (30–45 mins)
- ☐ Plan 1 joyful activity for YOU (even if it's small)
- ☐ Plan 1 day of lighter responsibility or intentional rest

Use this worksheet to plan your ideal week, taking into account your energy levels and life demands.

CHAPTER 4

Weekly Check-Ins & Adjustments

The Power of Weekly Reviews: Course-Correcting Without Self-Criticism

Let us examine our ways and test them, and let us return to the Lord.
— *Lamentations 3:40 (NIV)*

If daily routines are the heartbeat of your goals, then weekly check-ins are a crucial pause that keeps you aligned with God's purpose.

Life moves quickly, and it's easy to drift off course, not from a lack of desire, but from a lack of a positive, purposeful, focused routine. Intentional reflection is how we stop the cycle of burnout and return to balance. It's where we choose grace over guilt, curiosity over criticism, and alignment with God over anxiety.

I learned this the hard way. There were seasons when I was running on autopilot, serving everyone but myself, checking boxes but missing my heart's true desires. I had goals written down in beautiful journals, but months later, they hadn't moved. My schedule was full, but my soul was frustrated.

What changed everything? Weekly reflection. One small decision to pause, breathe, and reconnect with what actually mattered. Weekly reviews aren't just a productivity hack. They're a spiritual discipline. They're your chance to:

- Reconnect with your "why".
- Acknowledge the goodness of God and the growth in you.
- Give yourself grace without losing your focus.
- Make faith-led adjustments without shame.

Let's walk through this together, one gentle, grace-filled step at a time.

My Sunday Reset Ritual

On Sunday evenings, once the kitchen is clean and the house is settling down, I find my quiet space. Sometimes it's my bedroom with a diffuser and soft worship music. Other times, it's the closet (because motherhood isn't always Pinterest-perfect). I grab my journal and ask myself **five soul-centered questions:**

1. What were my wins this week?
2. What challenged me?
3. What did God teach me?
4. What needs adjusting, not abandoning?
5. How can I show up stronger (and softer) next week?

It's not about fixing myself. It's about observing with love. It's about recognizing that I'm growing. Reflection helps me parent more effectively, lead more effectively, and love myself more compassionately.

Celebrating Small Wins and Gracefully Facing Setbacks

As women, we are natural givers. We celebrate everyone else's progress but often forget to acknowledge our own. But dear friend, those small wins? They're a blessing and worth acknowledging.

✓ You swapped soda for water: Win.
✓ You set a boundary and kept it: Win.
✓ You spent 10 minutes in the Word: Win.
✓ You caught a spiral of negative thoughts and spoke Truth instead: **Major Win.**

Write them down. Make a "Wins List." Tape it to your mirror if necessary. These moments build momentum. They speak life back to you when your inner critic tries to speak defeat.

And what about the weeks that unravel right before your eyes? The ones where the plans fall apart, the energy runs low, and you're simply trying to catch your breath between the chaos? Those are the weeks that call for the most compassion, the ones that need an extra dose of grace, not guilt.

When everything feels off-track, don't spiral into discouragement and shame with thoughts like, "Why can't I get it together?" Instead, pause and gently ask, "Lord, what are You teaching me here?" or "What does faithfulness look like in this exact moment?"

That single mindset shift from pressure to an awareness of God's presence, from shame to surrender, will transform not only how you see the setback but also how you rise from it.

Even in the most challenging moments, you are still here. Still standing. Still able to move forward with God by your side. That alone is a miracle. You get to be here still to take on the challenge, and that's a blessing.

You're fully capable of conquering whatever you're facing. Look up, look to God for help, and get after it. With this transformation in your thinking, your life will move to the next level.

Remember, you are not failing, you are learning and growing. You are not weak; you are being strengthened. And with God's help, you will overcome. So take a deep breath, lift your head, fix your eyes on Jesus, and take the next step with courage.

Know that I've lifted you in prayer, I'm standing beside you in spirit, and I'm cheering you on every step you take forward!

The GRACE Method for Weekly Reviews

Let your week end not with pressure, but with peace. A weekly review isn't about scolding yourself; it's about realigning your soul, your schedule, and your spirit with what matters most. Just like a GPS quietly recalculates your route without condemnation, you can course-correct without guilt.

Use the GRACE Method to guide your review:

☐ **G: Ground Yourself in God's Truth:** Begin with Scripture. Anchor your week in what God says about you, not what your to-do list says about your performance. Open your Bible, even if it's just one verse. Let His truth remind you: You are loved. You are seen. You are not behind.

☐ **R: Reflect on Your Current Reality:** Take inventory. What actually happened this week, emotionally, spiritually, physically? What went well? What felt heavy? Be honest. No shame, just truth. This is your sacred space to process without pretending.

☐ **A: Act with Intentional Steps:** Look at the goals you set. What moved forward, and what didn't? What intentional step can you take this coming week to keep building momentum without burning out?

☐ **C: Create Consistent Systems:** Ask yourself: What small system or habit would make next week lighter? Course-correct. What needs to shift or soften? Maybe it's a 15-minute meal prep on Sundays. Maybe it's a new morning routine or a technology boundary. Your systems don't have to be fancy; they just need to serve you well.

☐ **E: Embrace Progress Over Perfection:** Celebrate what did get done. Don't wait until the big win. Praise God now for the little ones. Speak life over your next steps. Remind yourself: I'm growing. I'm learning. And God is with me in every imperfect step.

Let this GRACE-filled rhythm be a weekly date with yourself and God. It's not about judgment. It's about realignment. Just like GPS recalculates without scolding you, so can you. You're not failing. You're fine-tuning. Keep walking, one faithful step at a time.

Creating Accountability That Heals, Not Harms

We weren't meant to walk this journey alone. Jesus had an inner circle. So should you. Find one or two women who can hold space for your process. I call mine my prayer squad, the women who war with me in prayer, support me when I'm weak, come see about me when I'm on the verge of breaking, and walk with me in love. We check in every week, not just on goals, but on hearts as well. We celebrate, we cry, we pray, we conquer, and we rise.

Not sure who to ask? Start with prayer. God is faithful in bringing the right people at the right time. And remember: accountability isn't about performance. It's about presence. It's about being seen, supported, and reminded that you are not alone.

Applying the GRACE Method

This week, I challenge you to set aside 15 minutes for a grace-filled review. Light a candle. Play your favorite worship song. Ask the five questions. Celebrate the wins. Adjust what needs adjusting. Let grace meet you right where you are, and let God remind you that progress, even imperfect, is still holy and a blessing.

Reflection Questions:

1. What were three wins I can celebrate from this week?
2. Where did I experience resistance or frustration?
3. What did God reveal to me in that struggle?
4. What is one area I want to gently course-correct?
5. Who can I invite into my accountability circle this season?

A Prayer for You

Father,

Thank You for being patient with me as I grow. Help me to see myself through Your eyes: loved, called, growing, and purposeful. Teach me to celebrate progress and learn from setbacks. When I feel like giving up, whisper Your truth to my weary heart. Remind me that You're not looking for perfection. You're looking for my presence, and You're looking for me to be aware of and thankful for Your presence. Help me to pause, reflect, and realign with Your will each week.

In Jesus' name, Amen.

Remember, you're not starting over. You're starting stronger.

CHAPTER 5

Overcoming Obstacles & Staying Motivated

Overcoming Obstacles with Faith and Strategy

But one thing I do: Forgetting what is behind and straining toward what is ahead, I press on toward the goal to win the prize for which God has called me heavenward in Christ Jesus. — Philippians 3:13–14, NIV

Goal-setting often begins with so much hope and energy. The vision board is freshly pinned. Your journal pages are filled with faith declarations. Your heart is beating with purpose. And then...life hits. The notifications come. The responsibilities pile up. A sick child, an unexpected expense, a broken appliance, a hard phone call, a work crisis. Suddenly, that goal that once sparked joy now feels like a weight you're dragging uphill.

Let me lean in and whisper this to your soul: You are not broken because you're facing hard things. You are being beautifully, intentionally built through them. These aren't just disruptions in your life; these are divine developments. What may feel like a setback is often God's setup for something greater.

Growth doesn't always look graceful. It's often messy, stretching, and unseen. But it's purposeful. Pain in the process doesn't mean you've taken a wrong turn; it means God is still at work. You are growing. If you're still in process, that means your story isn't over. God is right there in the middle of your overwhelm, in the heart of your chaos, faithfully shaping you into a woman marked by resilience, clothed in wisdom, and grounded in unshakable faith.

The Myth of the Obstacle-Free Life

Here's something I wish more women knew in their heart and would say out loud: **Obstacles don't mean you're off track. They mean you're doing something worth fighting for.** I've coached countless women, and the difference between those who quit and those who grow is not the absence of hardship; **it's how they respond** when it gets hard.

Obstacles are not interruptions to your calling; they are invitations to deepen it.

Real-Life Story: When Everything Fell Apart

There have been seasons in my life when the weight felt unbearable, when it felt like the world was caving in around me, and I didn't know how I would make it through. In the first few years of my marriage (and motherhood), I experienced one devastating loss after another. My mother. All of my grandmothers. My mother-in-law. Even my grandmother-in-law. One by one, the women I had loved, leaned on, and looked to were gone. It was like the entire covering of generational wisdom, comfort, and presence had been ripped from my life all at once.

And to be honest, it broke something in me for some time. The realization that I would have to walk out the rest of my life journey without them felt like too much to bear.

There were days I could barely catch my breath, days when I felt like I was going through the motions with a smile on my face, while silently unraveling on the inside. Even the people closest to me couldn't fully grasp how heavy those years were. I was showing up for my family, but inwardly I was crawling.

Life continued and then came various emergencies, the kind that wake you in the middle of the night, the kind that shake your soul. I've held my breath in hospital rooms as my children fought through health crises. I've wrapped my arms around them after injuries on the field or court, or through overwhelming waves of anxiety. I've watched my husband suffer not one, but multiple strokes, back and forth from sitting by his hospital bedside for weeks and caring for all of our children, unsure of what life would look like on the other side. There were moments when fear tried to crush me. When the pressure of caregiving, marriage, parenting, community, finances, business, healthcare, and simply trying to keep it all together collided at once.

I remember one particular moment, sitting in my van outside the hospital. My body was still, but inside, I was sobbing. Tears silently rolling down my face my heart was screaming, "God, how am I supposed to do this? How do I keep going when everything around me feels like it's crumbling?"

Maybe you've asked Him the same questions. And here's the truth I've discovered. God always answers. Not always in lightning bolts, thunder or loud declarations, but in the quiet ways that reach deep. A gentle whisper to my spirit, a verse that lands exactly when I need it, the comforting words of a friend, or a wave of peace that makes no earthly sense but somehow steadies my soul. Over and over, He reminds me: "Your circumstances are not in conflict with your dreams; you are being refined through them. This is preparation. It's always a setup. This is all a part of your story of victory. Look up. Stay focused."

That truth became an anchor for me. Over time, I began referring to it as my "Crisis Protocol." It's not about pretending everything is okay when it's not. It's about remembering, even in the darkest moments, that God is still here. He is still writing your story. And He's still working all things together for your good.

*And we know that **in all things** God works for the good of those who love him, who have been called according to his purpose. —Romans 8:28, NIV.*

I had to learn how to pause in the middle of the chaos, lift my eyes, and ask, "God, what's the next right step?" Not ten steps ahead. Just one. And He always gives me what I need to take it.

So if you're in the middle of your own storm right now, if the weight feels unbearable and the way forward feels unclear, I want you to know this: You are not alone. God sees you. He's with you. And you will come through this, not just surviving, but stronger, wiser, and more victorious than you can even imagine.

When everything feels like it's falling apart, that's when you can be sure God is still holding it all together. So ask Him: "What's the next right step, Lord?" And take it. One faithful step at a time. Everything is going to be alright, eventually. Don't give up, keep trusting God, get up, and take the next step.

The 5 Most Common Obstacles Women Face

Over the years, I've seen the same patterns repeatedly. Here are five obstacles that threaten to derail progress, and how we can overcome them:

Obstacle 1: "I Don't Have Time"

This is the most common excuse, and trust me, I've said it too. But the truth is, it's not always about needing more hours. It's about needing more intention. You don't need more time; you need more faith in God and more faith concerning what you can do with the time you have.

Strategy: Time Audit + Micro-Moments:

Try tracking your day in 15-minute increments for just 3 days. You'll likely uncover hidden pockets of time you can reclaim. Complain less, and take action more.

Micro-Moments to Maximize:

- 5 minutes: Pray, stretch, gratitude journal
- 10 minutes: Listen to a podcast, read a page of a growth book
- 15 minutes: Brain dump, clean a space, write a quick goal update

Ephesians 5:15-16 reminds us to "make the most of every opportunity." With God, even your smallest windows of time can move mountains.

Obstacle 2: Energy Depletion

You may not be short on time, but you might be running on empty. Your dreams need your energy, not just your calendar.

Strategy: Energy Budgeting + Restoration Rituals

Create a weekly energy budget. Label tasks by how much they drain you (1-5 points). Don't overload your days with too many 5-point activities.

Restoration Routines and Rituals:

- 5-minute reset: A worship song, step outside, deep breathing
- 15-minute recharge: A cup of tea, scripture journaling, mindful movement
- 30-minute restore: A bath, nature walk, or call with a trusted friend

Obstacle 3: Guilt and Perfectionism

You feel bad for even wanting something for yourself. You're stuck believing you have to do it all perfectly, or not at all.

Strategy: Give Yourself Permission

Say this out loud with me:

- "I give myself permission to pursue what God placed in my heart."
- "I give myself permission to rest."
- "I give myself permission to grow, even if it's messy."

Progress is always better than perfection. Always.

Obstacle 4: Fear and Self-Doubt

Fear whispers, "What if you fail? What if you're not good enough?" But fear is a liar, and faith gets the final word.

Strategy: Faith Declarations + Fear Inventory

Write your fears. Then write what God says about them. Speak the truth until your soul believes it.

Examples to write, speak, and meditate on:

For God did not give us a spirit of timidity or cowardice or fear, but {He has given us a spirit} of power and of love and of sound judgment and personal discipline {abilities that result in a calm, well-balanced mind and self-control}.
—2 Timothy 1:7, AMP.

I can do all things {which He has called me to do} through Him who strengthens and empowers me {to fulfill His purpose—I am self-sufficient in Christ's sufficiency; I am ready for anything and equal to anything through Him who infuses me with inner strength and confident peace. —Philippians 4:13, AMP

Obstacle 5: Life Disruptions

Sometimes the curveballs keep coming. Illness. Grief. Financial shifts. Unexpected chaos.

Strategy: Crisis Protocol + Minimum Viable Progress

Ask:

- God, what is the next right step?
- What is one thing I can still do today?
- What's the smallest step that still moves me forward?

Even a whispered prayer, a short list, or a 2-minute journal entry counts.

The Spiritual Side of Struggle

For our struggle is not against flesh and blood {contending only with physical opponents}, but against the rulers, against the powers, against the world forces of this {present} darkness, against the spiritual forces of wickedness in the heavenly (supernatural) places. —Ephesians 6:12, AMP

Some obstacles are logistical. Others are deeply spiritual. When you start stepping into your purpose, don't be surprised if resistance shows up. The enemy doesn't fight what isn't threatening. Your obedience is powerful.

Spiritual Warfare Plan:

1. Armor up: Ephesians 6:10–18.
2. Stay surrounded: Ask your circle to pray.
3. Declare the truth of God's Word out loud daily.

If the enemy is attacking, it's because your breakthrough matters.

Emergency Motivation Toolkit

On the days you feel like giving up, use these:

When you feel like quitting:
- [ ] Read your "why".
- [ ] Call your accountability partner.
- [ ] Do ONE small thing for your goal.

When you feel overwhelmed:
☐ Take 10 deep breaths.
☐ Focus on just today.
☐ Surrender your worry to God.

When you feel discouraged:
☐ Journal your progress.
☐ Celebrate one small win.
☐ Read Romans 8:28 out loud.

"And we know {with great confidence} that God {who is deeply concerned about us} causes all things to work together {as a plan} for good for those who love God, to those who are called according to His plan and purpose." —Romans 8:28, AMP.

Remember, any failure you face isn't final. It's fertilizer. Let God use it to grow you.

Mindset Shifts That Keep You Going

"This is hard"   ⇨   "This is stretching me."
"I'm not good at this" ⇨   "I'm learning."
"I failed"   ⇨   "I'm growing."

Every time you rise again, you strengthen your faith muscle. Keep showing up.

Applying the GRACE Method: Overcoming Obstacles & Staying Motivated

Obstacles are part of every breakthrough story, but they don't have to be the end of yours. Use the GRACE Method to process what's weighing you down and reignite your momentum with faith and focus:

☐ **G: Ground Yourself in God's Truth:** Open your Bible and let God's promises speak louder than your problems. Meditate on scriptures like Philippians 4:13 or Isaiah 41:10. Remind your heart that setbacks don't disqualify you. God's grace is your strength.

I can do all things through Christ who strengthens me.

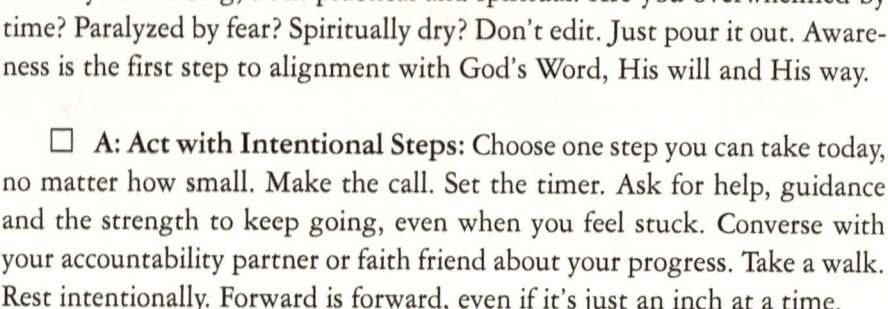

— Philippians 4:13, NKJV

Fear not, for I am with you; Be not dismayed, for I am your God. I will strengthen you, Yes, I will help you, I will uphold you with My righteous right hand.
— Isaiah 41:10, NKJV

☐ **R: Reflect on Your Current Reality:** Get honest. Journal the road-blocks you're facing, both practical and spiritual. Are you overwhelmed by time? Paralyzed by fear? Spiritually dry? Don't edit. Just pour it out. Awareness is the first step to alignment with God's Word, His will and His way.

☐ **A: Act with Intentional Steps:** Choose one step you can take today, no matter how small. Make the call. Set the timer. Ask for help, guidance and the strength to keep going, even when you feel stuck. Converse with your accountability partner or faith friend about your progress. Take a walk. Rest intentionally. Forward is forward, even if it's just an inch at a time.

☐ **C: Create Consistent Systems:** What tiny routine or tool could help you overcome this obstacle next time it shows up? Whether it's a daily declaration, setting phone boundaries, or planning your week on Sundays; consistency builds confidence.

☐ **E: Embrace Progress Over Perfection:** Celebrate the fact that you're still here and still trying. Thank God for every small win, especially the imperfect ones. Motivation isn't about hype. It's about hope. And your hope is not in your hustle, but in Him.

When life feels like it's slowing you down, this is how you keep going: with grace, truth, and just one faithful step at a time. You've got this, sis. And God's got you.

Reflection Questions:

1. What has been my most consistent obstacle this season?
2. How have I been responding, through faith or frustration?
3. What small shift can I make this week to reclaim my time, energy, or mindset?
4. Who can I ask to pray with and support me?

Prayer for Overcoming Obstacles

Father God,

Thank You for reminding me that obstacles don't disqualify me; they prepare me. Help me to see challenges as divine classroom moments, where I am refined, not rejected. Give me the grace to keep going, the wisdom to know what matters most, and the strength to press on when life feels overwhelming. Remind me that I am never alone and that You are working all things together for my good.

In Jesus' name, Amen.

You're not falling behind. You're growing into the woman God designed you to be, resilient, faithful, and unstoppable in grace.

CHAPTER 6

The Role of Gratitude and Affirmations

The Gratitude Shift: Speaking Life into Your Everyday

Give thanks in all circumstances; for this is God's will for you in Christ Jesus.
— 1 Thessalonians 5:18, NIV.

Gratitude and affirmations may sound simple, but don't underestimate their power. These two habits are like spiritual vitamins: small doses each day that nourish the soul, strengthen the heart, and gently rewire your mind toward peace and joy. Gratitude shifts your perspective. Affirmations shift your narrative. Together, they help you hold onto hope and identity when everything around you feels like it's spinning out of control.

I want to start with a confession. There have been times and whole seasons in my life when gratitude was the last thing on my mind. I didn't want to say another Bible verse or affirmation. I didn't want to hear someone tell me to "just be thankful." I was tired. I was hurting. I felt unseen, overwhelmed, betrayed, and stretched to the edge of my strength. Life kept asking more of me, and I had no reserves left. And yet, in that place of exhaustion, I chose to say three small words each morning: "Thank You, God."

It started small. I thanked Him for breath in my lungs, for a new day, the gift of a new sunrise, the warmth of water on my skin, the quiet comfort of morning coffee, and the precious weight of my children's hugs. Not because life was easy or perfect; it wasn't. But because I needed God to meet me right there, in the middle of the mess.

Gratitude became my invitation for His presence to sit with me in the imperfection. And although my circumstances didn't change overnight, something within me began to shift. My mind cleared. My heart softened. My perspective lifted. Little by little, peace began to bloom again where fear had been. Joy peeked through the cracks of weariness. And slowly, strength returned. Not from striving, but from remembering I wasn't walking through this alone. God was right there. And with Him beside me, I could begin again.

Why Gratitude Works: The Science and Impact on Our Lives

Modern research is finally catching up to what God has said all along.

Studies show that consistent gratitude:

- Increases happiness and reduces depression
- Improves sleep and strengthens immunity
- Enhances relationships
- Builds emotional resilience

But for us as women of faith, gratitude is more than a mental health practice; it's a form of worship. It's how we enter His gates. It's how we remind ourselves, in the thick of womanhood, motherhood, marriage, ministry, or just messy life, that God is still good, and we are still held.

Enter His gates with thanksgiving and His courts with praise; give thanks to Him and praise His name. — Psalm 100:4, NIV.

Real-Life Gratitude in the Middle of a Storm

There was a season when the weight of life nearly swallowed me whole. One of my children was walking through something that broke my heart in places I didn't even know could ache. My husband was in the hospital again, and I was stretched thin, trying to be strong, keep everyone fed, hold everyone's emotions, and somehow not fall apart myself.

I remember sitting in the quiet early one morning, my Bible open but blurry through the tears. I was clutching a pillow like it was the only thing holding me together. And through broken sobs, I whispered, "God... I don't even know what to thank You for today."

But the Holy Spirit met me there. In that silent moment of unraveling, I felt a gentle whisper in my spirit:

"Start with what remains. Start with what (or who) still breathes in your life. Start with what still brings warmth. Start with what still holds you."

So I did. I began to speak:

- Thank You for breath in my lungs.
- Thank You for the comfort of warm coffee in my hands.
- Thank You for the meal I had the strength to prepare last night.
- Thank You for sparing my husband's life.
- Thank You for the lives of my children.
- Thank You for my child's laughter, even if it was brief.
- Thank You that even in the hurt, You haven't left me. You're still here.
- Thank You for being the lifter of my head, the lover of my soul (Psalm 3:3, Isaiah 38:17).
- Thank you for being my Advocate, Intercessor, Counselor, Strengthener, and my Comforter (John 14:16, AMP).

That small shift, that significant pause, became my anchor.

No, it didn't erase the storm, but it became an umbrella in the downpour. It reminded me that I don't need perfect circumstances to have a grateful heart. I just need to look for what still reflects God's presence, and what demonstrates His power, even in the middle of the mess. Because He sees every tear. He honors every whispered prayer. And even on the hardest days, gratitude brings me back to the truth: I am not alone. God is with me, and His goodness still remains.

The 4 in 5 Gratitude Formula

Here's a simple gratitude practice you can start today:

1. One small moment from today you're grateful for
2. One person who blessed you
3. One way you saw God provide or show up
4. One thing you're trusting God with for tomorrow

Just five minutes. Just four prompts. However, this formula has helped me, as well as many of my coaching clients, shift from exhaustion to empowerment.

Affirmations: The Voice That Shapes Your Victory

What we say to ourselves matters. We become what we repeatedly believe. And too often, our internal soundtrack plays like this:

- "I'm a failure."
- "I'll never be enough."
- "She's doing it better than I ever could."

Sis, those are not your truths. They are lies. And it's time to replace them with what God says.

Affirmations are more than feel-good phrases. When rooted in scripture, they become declarations of identity. Every time you say, "I am chosen. I am loved. I am strong," you are not pretending. You are partnering with Heaven to shift your inner world and align with the truth of God's Word.

My Mirror Moment

There was a time in my life when betrayal shattered me so deeply, I felt it in my body like an earthquake. It felt like someone had punched me in my stomach and my face at the same time. The kind of pain that leaves you breathless, not just emotionally, but physically. Anxiety wrapped itself around my chest, and every part of me felt like it was unraveling. I don't know if you've ever experienced deception so sharp that your body goes into shock, but I did. It left me with cold chills that I couldn't shake, and it left me questioning everything: my worth, my purpose, my calling, my voice, and even whether I was truly loved at all.

On some days, the only prayer I could whisper was, "God, please calm my nervous system. Please comfort my soul." And that was all I had.

Every night, I cried myself to sleep. And every morning, I forced myself to stand in front of the mirror, with swollen eyes and a trembling voice, and I began to speak. Not because I felt strong, but because I needed to remember I still had a voice, and that voice had power. I spoke to the daughter of God in the mirror:
- "I am loved."
- "I am covered."
- "I am chosen."
- "God is with me, and I am equipped for today."

At first, nothing seemed to change. I still couldn't sleep. My thoughts still raced, and my body still shivered. But I kept showing up, kept declaring truth over myself, until something started to shift. Slowly and quietly, the words began to sink in deeper. My heart began to believe what my mouth was saying. My soul caught up to my confession. And slowly, peace found its way back in.

Rest came, not because the pain disappeared overnight, but because I began to remember who I was... and even more importantly, *who God is*. That's the power of affirmations rooted in His Word. They don't mask the pain or pretend it away. They minister to your soul when your feelings scream louder than your faith. When life circumstances come to take your breath and voice away, it's time for you to scream back. Speaking truth over myself each day became more than a habit; it became my healing.

Life (and people) tried to break me, and honestly, part of me knew I'd never be the same again. But I made a decision: I wouldn't stay shattered. I gathered the broken pieces of my heart and laid them at the feet of the One who knows how to restore what feels beyond repair. I let God pick up what I couldn't carry and rebuild me from the inside out, stronger, wiser, softer, but more powerful than ever before.

When God speaks, and you finally pause long enough to listen, something shifts. You begin to see everything differently. What once looked like the end becomes a beginning. What was meant to destroy you becomes the very thing that frees you. That breaking point? It wasn't the end of me. It was the beginning of something purposeful, freeing, and holy.

If God allows something to break down, it's never to leave you in pieces. It's because He intends to build something stronger, more radiant, and more aligned with the future He's written for you. And sis, what tried to break you? It only succeeded in breaking the limits off of your life that were never meant to be there in the first place.

Create Your Own Faith-Filled Affirmation

1. **Identify the lie:** "I'm not strong enough."
2. **Find the truth:** "The Lord is my strength and my shield." (Psalm 28:7)
3. **Affirm the truth:** "I am strong in the Lord and fully equipped for today."

You can do this with every area where doubt, fear, or insecurity tries to sneak in. Let God's Word be louder.

Daily Practice: The Morning 10-Minute Shift

- ☐ Gratitude: 3 specific things you're thankful for
- ☐ Affirmations: 1-3 truth-filled "I am" statements
- ☐ Scripture: One verse to carry with you

Try it tomorrow morning. Watch how your mood, mindset, and motivation shift before your coffee even finishes brewing.

Applying the GRACE Method: Gratitude & Affirmations

Gratitude isn't just a feel-good habit; it's a spiritual weapon. Affirmations rooted in God's truth help rewire the inner dialogue that's kept many women stuck in cycles of doubt, discouragement, or defeat. Use the GRACE Method to let both become part of your healing rhythm.

☐ **G: Ground Yourself in God's Truth:** Start by anchoring your heart in Scripture. Choose a verse that reminds you of who God is and who you are because of Him. (Try Psalm 103:1–5, Romans 8:28, or Isaiah 43:1.) Write it where you'll see it often. Let His truth reset your mindset.

Praise for the Lord's Mercies: "Bless the Lord, O my soul; And all that is within me, bless His holy name! Bless the Lord, O my soul, And forget not all His benefits: Who forgives all your iniquities, Who heals all your diseases, Who redeems your life from destruction, Who crowns you with lovingkindness and tender mercies, Who satisfies your mouth with good things, So that your youth is renewed like the eagle's."
— Psalm 103:1–5, NKJV

And we know that all things work together for good to those who love God, to those who are the called according to His purpose.
—Romans 8:28, NKJV

...Fear not, for I have redeemed you; I have called you by your name; You are Mine.
— Isaiah 43:1, NKJV

☐ **R: Reflect on Your Current Reality:** Where are you most tempted to complain, compare, or spiral into negativity? Where does your self-talk still carry the sound of shame, fear, or burnout? Identify the areas of your life that need the light of gratitude and the voice of truth.

☐ **A: Act with Intentional Steps:** Write your "4-in-5" list: Four things you're grateful for in five minutes or less. Speak your affirmations aloud, even if your voice shakes. Words have power, and yours matter. Declare what God says about you until your heart begins to believe it again.

☐ **C: Create Consistent Systems:** Establish a simple 5-minute daily ritual (morning, midday, or night) where you pause, reflect, speak, and give thanks. Whether it's through journaling, sticky notes on your mirror, or quiet prayer while driving, consistency builds a new default for your thoughts.

☐ **E: Embrace Progress Over Perfection:** This is about rewiring, not rushing. If your thoughts shifted *even once today* toward hope, that's victory. Celebrate those micro-moments where your mindset aligned with heaven. This isn't performance; it's transformation through practice and grace.

You're not just reciting words; you're rebuilding your inner world with truth. Gratitude grounds you. Affirmations shift you. And God's presence transforms everything in between. Keep going, sis. Your soul is beginning to bloom.

Reflection Questions:

1. Where have I struggled to find gratitude lately?
2. What lie have I been believing that needs to be replaced with God's truth?
3. How does it feel to speak life over myself?
4. What can I thank God for today, even if it's small?

A Prayer for Gratitude

God,

Thank You for being faithful, even when my circumstances feel heavy. Help me develop a heart that sees Your goodness, even in the ordinary. Remind me that my words have power and that when I speak life, I partner with You to bring healing and hope into my day. Replace every lie with truth, every fear with faith, and every heaviness with hope. Let gratitude rise in me like the dawn, and let my words reflect Your heart. Let my heart be positioned to listen. Thank You for the grace to grow.

In Jesus' name, Amen.

Next: We'll walk through how to assess the key areas of your life and begin building habits, routines, and a rhythm that all align with your vision, your values, and God's best for you. Get ready, sis. The shift is just beginning.

CHAPTER 7

Transforming Key Areas of Life

Taking Inventory of Your Sacred Space and Territory

The thief comes only in order to steal and kill and destroy. I came that they may
have and enjoy life, and have it in abundance {to the full, till it overflows}.
—John 10:10, AMP

Let me pause here, beautiful sister, and speak directly to your heart. You weren't made just to survive life; you were made to thrive. You were created for a life that is abundant, meaningful, joyful, and uniquely yours. I know what it feels like to run on empty, to be juggling the demands of motherhood, marriage, community, faith, and purpose, and still feel like you're missing something essential. So let me assure you: your life matters, your joy matters, and every part of who you are deserves to be nurtured with intention, compassion, and grace.

Transformation doesn't begin with striving. It starts with surrender. It begins with giving God full access and saying, "Lord, here I am. Show me what You see. Teach me where to begin." It starts with granting yourself permission to breathe again, to dream again, and to heal what's been buried under the busyness of survival. You don't need to fix everything all at once. But you can begin somewhere. And that somewhere is right here, right now.

I often tell women to imagine their life as a garden, with different plots representing different areas of life: your faith, your family, your finances, your health, your calling, and more. Some plots may be blooming with fruit, others may be overgrown, and some may still be waiting for seeds to be planted. And that's okay. You're not behind. You're just entering a new season. And here's the most essential truth: you don't have to obsess over watering every plot at the same time. Just pick the one that needs you the most right now. Tend to it faithfully and then move to the next. Progress will follow.

Let me tell you about a moment that shifted my thinking. I was sitting across from Erica, a successful business executive and mom of three, as she wept in frustration. "I'm winning at work and failing at home, or winning at home and dropping the ball at work. I can't seem to get it right," she said through tears. "I just need to know where I actually stand."

Her words hit me like a bolt of lightning because I've felt that too. That pressure. That pull. That exhaustion from just knowing that winning in one area many times means feeling like you're losing big time in another. And it was in that moment that the Life Assessment Tool was born. A grace-filled framework to help women gain clarity, honesty, and hope about where they are and where God wants to take them.

Most assessments feel cold and clinical. They make you feel like you're failing if you're not hitting every mark. But this tool is different. It's not about achievements or perfection, it's about alignment. Alignment with your faith, alignment with your values, alignment with the vision God has placed within you. It will help you look gently but truthfully at each area of your life, not so you can judge yourself, but so you can support yourself better, with love, wisdom, and intention.

We'll walk through *12 key areas of life.* These are the same areas featured in the *"Create the Life You Want Now: 90-Day Goal Journal"* (available on Amazon). Each area will invite you to pause, reflect, and renew. You'll have the chance to assess yourself honestly, not to feel shame, but to see clearly and choose growth.

These 12 sacred life areas are:
1. **Spiritual Health:** How connected you are to God and your faith
2. **Personal Goals:** Your dreams, desires, and goals as a woman
3. **Marriage & Family:** Your closest relationships and family dynamics
4. **Parenting:** How you lead, nurture, and support your children
5. **Relationships:** Your friendships, boundaries, and community
6. **Career & Business:** The work you do and the calling you walk in
7. **Education & Growth:** Your learning, development, and mindset
8. **Physical Health:** Your strength, wellness, and self-care habits
9. **Financial Health:** How you manage, steward, and plan your finances
10. **Your Environment:** Your home, routines, and surroundings
11. **Joy & Fun:** The ways you rest, play, laugh, and recharge

12. **Giving:** The overflow of generosity and impact you share with others.

You'll find detailed assessment questions and journal reflection questions for each section inside the companion journal. For now, I just want you to breathe deeply and believe this: *you can create a life you genuinely love.* One that feels healed and whole. Not because you're doing it all perfectly, but because you're choosing to do it prayerfully.

* You are not behind.
* You are not broken.
* You are building, rebuilding, and becoming.

Let's begin this sacred assessment, not with judgment, but with joy, and with gratitude for the opportunity. You're not just checking boxes. You're checking in with your heart. And that, my friend, is purposeful work.

Applying the GRACE Method: Transforming Key Areas of Your Life

Transformation doesn't happen all at once; it unfolds moment by moment, choice by choice, step by spirit-filled step. Whether you're navigating a season of change in your relationships, health, finances, or emotional well-being, the GRACE Method will help you make intentional progress with compassion and faith.

☐ **G: Ground Yourself in God's Truth:** Begin by remembering who you are and Whose you are. You are not too far behind. You are not too broken or too late. You are not broken at all, you are in the process of being built. You are seen, known, and loved by a God who specializes in renewal. Meditate on truths like Isaiah 43:19 or Philippians 1:6. Let His Word remind you: your transformation is already in motion.

Behold, I will do a new thing, Now it shall spring forth; Shall you not know it? I will even make a road in the wilderness And rivers in the desert.
— Isaiah 43:19, NKJV

Being confident of this very thing, that He who has begun a good work in you will complete it until the day of Jesus Christ;
— Philippians 1:6, NKJV

☐ **R: Reflect on Your Current Reality:** Take a gentle inventory of your life. What areas feel full of light and life? Which ones feel dry, neglected, or chaotic? Don't rush to fix, just notice. Invite God into the reflection. Ask Him to show you what He wants to revive, prune, or breathe new life into. This isn't about shame; it's about awareness and spiritual alignment.

☐ **A: Act with Intentional Steps:** Pick just one area to focus on for the next 30 days. It might be your morning routine, your physical health, emotional boundaries, or decluttering your home. Don't overcommit. Small, consistent actions, like 10 minutes a day, create meaningful momentum. Start where you are, and let faith lead the way.

☐ **C: Create Consistent Systems:** Transformation thrives in rhythm, not rush. Establish a weekly habit of checking in with yourself and with God. Journal your growth. Pray over your progress. Set a recurring time each week to reflect on what's working and what needs grace. Anchor yourself in routine, not pressure.

☐ **E: Embrace Progress Over Perfection:** You're not called to flawless progress, you're called to faithful progress. Some days will feel messy or slow, but that doesn't mean you're failing. Celebrate every inch of growth. Acknowledge every step forward, even the quiet ones. God isn't measuring your speed; He's walking with you in your surrender.

Your life doesn't have to be perfectly polished to be holy ground. Let this be your season of consecrated transformation, where grace leads, faith sustains, and God meets you right where you are, ready to walk you into what's next.

Reflection Questions:

1. Which of the 12 life areas feels strongest for you right now? Why?
2. Which area feels the most neglected or overwhelming?

3. How does your current season of life affect your ability to prioritize certain areas?
4. What would it look like to invite God into your weakest area today?
5. How can you show yourself grace as you begin this process?

A Prayer for the Journey:

Father God,

Thank You for the beautiful woman who is reading this. Thank You for her courage to pause and reflect, even when life feels full and messy. Remind her that she's not alone in this journey, that You are walking with her, cheering her on, and equipping her to become all You've called her to be. Help her to see her life with fresh eyes. Give her clarity where there is confusion, hope where there is heaviness, and joy in the areas that need restoration. May she sense Your presence in every breath, every step, and every brave decision she makes to grow. Let this be a purposeful reset. Let this be the beginning of a life more abundant.

In Jesus' name, amen.

Let's keep going, friend. The best is still ahead.

CHAPTER 8

Spiritual Health: Faith Over Fear, Connection Over Chaos

Spiritual Health: Your Foundation for Everything Else

Seek first the Kingdom of God and His righteousness, and all these things will be given to you as well. — Matthew 6:33, NIV

It always amazes me how the most powerful transformations begin in the quietest of places. Early one morning, long before the sun rose and the demands of the day came calling, I sat with my devotional, Bible, and a lukewarm cup of coffee, weary from a season that had left me emotionally tattered. As I exhaled a whispered prayer, more like a sigh than a sentence, I felt God gently speak back, *"Start here. With Me."*

Your spiritual life is the soil from which every other part of your life grows. When that soil is rich and nourished, your relationships, goals, and daily responsibilities have room to flourish. But when your spirit is dry or disconnected, even your best efforts in work, parenting, marriage, or health can leave you feeling exhausted and drained. This isn't about adding more to your already full to-do list. It's about anchoring your to-do list in the One who restores your soul, offers rest, renews your strength, and brings purpose and peace to every part of your journey.

The Three Pillars of Spiritual Health

Spiritual vitality rests on three foundational pillars: Prayer, Scripture, and Service. These are not religious checklists. They are just sacred rhythms that tether your soul to God in real-time.

Pillar 1: Transforming Your Prayer Life

Prayer is not a religious chore; it's your soul's oxygen. It is the lifeline to your Creator. It's the safe space where your tears are understood, put in God's bottle, and recorded in His book (Psalm 56:8, AMP). It's where your silence is heard, and your fears are held by the One who already knows you completely and loves you still.

For so many women, especially moms, caregivers, leaders, and dreamers, life becomes a nonstop cycle of giving, fixing, showing up, and holding it all together. And yet, under all that effort, there's a quiet ache:

Does anyone see me?
Is anyone holding me while I hold everyone else?

This is where prayer becomes everything.

Prayer is not about having the right words; it's about bringing the real concerns of your heart to God. You don't need eloquence, you need honesty. There is no perfect script. You can pray through tears on your bathroom floor, whisper gratitude over a kitchen sink, or ask God for strength while sitting in a carpool line with a racing mind and a tired heart.

Start simple: Let your first morning breath say, "Thank You for this day." Before your feet even hit the floor, surrender your schedule, your stress, and your soul. Give God your concerns, your hopes, and your day. End your night with reflection: *"Where did I see You today?"* Invite God into the car rides, the meetings, the meal prep, and the mess.

Tie prayer to your everyday routines. Talk to Him while brushing your teeth, journal your anxieties and hopes, or play worship music while folding laundry. When you're in survival mode, remember: to simply pray while brushing your teeth, worship while driving, and pause now and then to write in your journal to talk to God. Authentic and consistent connection, not length, is what fuels intimacy.

God doesn't need polished prayers; He wants your presence. When you show up, even with a broken heart or distracted mind, He shows up with peace that surpasses understanding. You don't need hours. You need intention. Five minutes of real connection can shift the entire atmosphere of your day. Prayer doesn't just change your circumstances; it changes you. It calms your nervous system, centers your emotions, and reminds your spirit that you are never alone.

So if you're feeling weary, if life has you stretched thin and running on empty, don't push harder. Pause. Let prayer be the place you come to breathe, to be held, and to be restored. Not because it's another task to check off your list, but because your soul was designed to connect with the Source of peace, power, love, and clarity. In that sacred space, God doesn't just listen; He strengthens. He pours into you what the world drains out.

Through prayer, He offers sound judgment, supernatural wisdom, and personal discipline: abilities that lead to a calm, well-balanced mind and the self-control you've been longing for (2 Timothy 1:7, AMP). Prayer is not just where you speak; it's where you receive. And what you receive can change everything.

Pillar 2: Making Scripture Come Alive

Scripture is your daily bread. And like any meal, it doesn't have to be fancy to nourish you.

Use The FEAST Method:

This isn't about checking a box. It's about feeding your spirit and hearing God's voice, one bite at a time.

F: Find a Passage: Start small. Don't pressure yourself to read a whole chapter. Sometimes, one verse is precisely what God wants to use to speak to your heart that day.

E: Examine the Context: What's happening in the story? Who's speaking, and why? Understanding the backdrop of a passage opens the door for deeper revelation.

A: Ask Questions: What does this reveal about God's character? What is He showing me about my own heart? What promise is He inviting me to believe today?

S: Seek Application: Scripture is alive, meant to be lived, not just learned. Ask, "How does this apply to what I'm facing right now?" Let the Holy Spirit guide you into action, even if it's simply choosing peace over panic or hope over fear.

T: Talk to God: Let your study end in conversation. Prayer seals what God is planting. Thank Him, ask for help, and invite Him to keep speaking as you move through your day.

You don't have to be a Bible scholar to encounter God. You just need a willing heart and a few quiet minutes. If you're new to this, I recommend starting with the Psalms, which meet you in your emotions, or the Gospel of John, which intimately reveals the heart of Jesus. Choose one verse. Write it down. Sit with it. Ask God to meet you there, and He will.

Remember, the goal isn't perfection; it's presence. When Scripture becomes more than words on a page, when it becomes a conversation, a comfort, a correction, and a call to action, it will shift everything in your life. Scripture doesn't just inform you. It transforms you.

And here's the beautiful promise: the same God who breathed those words thousands of years ago is still breathing life into your story today.

So, let's quickly review the FEAST method:

F: Find a Passage: Don't worry about reading chapters. Sometimes one verse is enough.

E: Examine the Context: Understand what's happening in the passage.

A: Ask Questions: What does this show me about God? What does He want me to know?

S: Seek Application: What does this mean for my life today?

T: Talk to God: Let your study end with prayer.

Write down what stirs your heart. God will meet you in the Word.

Pillar 3: Living Out Your Faith Through Service

Service isn't about platforms or perfection; it's about your presence with people. It's about love that moves. And it often starts in the quiet corners of our lives, not the spotlight.

For so many women, especially those of us who carry the weight of nurturing, managing, healing, and holding it all together, life can feel like a never-ending to-do list. You're running on fumes, and now someone's telling you to serve? You might be thinking, "I can barely get through my own day. What do I even have to give?"

But here's what I've learned: service is not about what others think you should be doing. It's about the little or large actions that God guides you to do for others each day. It's between you and God. Service doesn't deplete you when it flows from a surrendered heart; it fills you. It roots you in purpose when you're tempted to spiral into anxiety. It reconnects you to who you truly are when life tries to bury your identity under the weight of chores, grief, or burnout.

God never meant for service to be one more box to check. He meant it to be a lifeline. A way for us to sow and pour the love we've been given into others, one small act at a time.

Start Where You Are, With What You Have

You don't need to fly across the globe or start a nonprofit tomorrow to make an impact. Sometimes, the most powerful thing you can do is text a hurting friend and tell her she's not alone. Sometimes it looks like praying silently while folding socks. Sometimes it's bringing soup to a new mama, or sitting quietly with someone who's grieving.

If you're in a busy or seemingly broken season, especially if your energy is low, your heart is heavy, or your plate is full, let service be simple and Spirit-led.

- Pray for someone in secret.
- Write a note of encouragement.
- Speak a kind word to your child or your coworker.
- Bring peace into a tense room.

God sees the hidden things. He blesses the willing heart, not just the visible effort.

But if you're in a season with more capacity and resources, start asking: "Where is God stirring my heart?" Do you feel drawn to mentor a younger woman? To start a small group? To lead a prayer circle or offer your testimony? What moves your spirit? What injustice, what pain, what longing in others breaks your heart? That's often where your calling lies.

Creating Routines of Grace

The most spiritually vibrant women I know aren't the ones with endless free time. They're the ones who protect their peace, stay soft-hearted, and move slowly and intentionally. They're not running; they're rooted.

Here's a rhythm you can begin right now:

☐ Morning (5 Minutes): Scripture + prayer. Ask, "God, help me see You today."

☐ Midday (30 Seconds): Deep breath. "You're here, Lord. Help me continue with peace."

☐ Evening (5 Minutes): Reflect and give thanks. "God, where did I see You today?"

These micro-habits anchor you when your emotions feel loud and your days feel long. And over time, they shape a life that walks with God, not just for Him.

When God Feels Distant

If your spirit feels dry, if the Word feels dull, prayer feels hard, or worship feels like going through the motions, nothing is wrong with you. You are human. And you are not alone.

Spiritual dryness isn't a sign of failure. It's a cue to slow down, rest, lean in, and listen deeper.

Ask gently:

- Is there unconfessed hurt or unforgiveness weighing me down?
- Am I letting busyness or bitterness crowd out intimacy?
- Have I paused long enough just to be still?

If you're walking through depression, anxiety, grief, or trauma, please seek help. Therapy, community, and support are not signs of weakness; they are essential for growth and well-being. They are often the exact tools God uses to carry us through our trials. Sometimes, the most spiritual thing you can do is ask for help.

The Fruit of a Spiritually Anchored Life

When your spirit is watered, when you're showing up daily with God, even imperfectly, you will notice:

- You worry less and trust more.

- You begin to respond with grace instead of reacting in fear.
- You hear God's voice in the middle of the chaos.
- You discover joy that isn't tied to your circumstances.
- You start living on purpose, even in the most mundane moments.

When life circumstances keep you up and you find yourself in tears in the bathroom at 3:15 AM, you come to realize the turning point doesn't always come with fireworks or fanfare. It comes when you whisper, "God, I need You," and realize that He's been right there the entire time. In the stillness. In the struggle. In the service.

God isn't looking for perfect women. He's looking for present ones. Present in their homes, present in their pain, present in His presence. You don't have to hustle to earn holiness, just open your heart to live God's Word and follow His voice one faithful step at a time.

Applying the GRACE Method to Your Spiritual Life

Your relationship with God isn't just another thing to squeeze into your planner; it is the very foundation that sustains everything else. If your soul has been feeling dry, distracted, or disconnected, don't despair. You don't need to start over. You simply need a spiritual reset rooted in grace, not guilt. Let the GRACE Method help you gently realign and rekindle your spiritual health.

☐ **G: Ground Yourself in God's Truth:** Begin your day by grounding yourself in who God is and who He says you are. Before the world speaks into your life, let His Word speak first. Open your Bible, even if just for a verse, and ask: "What truth do I need to carry today?" Remember, you are not behind. You are deeply loved, fully seen, and always invited into God's presence.

My flesh and my heart may fail, but God is the strength of my heart and my portion forever. — Psalm 73:26 , NIV

"You will keep in perfect peace all who trust in You, all whose thoughts are fixed on You." —Isaiah 26:3, NLT

These verses are to remind you that your spiritual strength doesn't come from your perfection, but from God's presence. Even in weakness or chaos, you can root yourself in His peace and *faithful* character.

☐ **R: Reflect on Your Current Reality:** How is your soul, really? Sit with God in that question. No filters, no pressure, just honesty. What's weighing heavy? What's stirring underneath the surface? Let your prayer life become a dedicated space for reflection, where you can talk to your Father as a daughter, not a performer, coming back to an awareness of His presence in and around you.

☐ **A: Act with Intentional Steps:** Don't wait for perfect conditions to reconnect with God. Start where you are. Tie prayer to everyday habits: while brushing your teeth, folding laundry, or walking outside. Choose one intentional step to nurture your spirit each day. Maybe it's five minutes of worship music, journaling a prayer, or meditating on one Psalm. Small steps create heaven-kissed momentum.

☐ **C: Create Consistent Systems:** Spiritual health thrives with rhythm. Build a personal routine that gently invites God into your day: a verse in the morning, a breath prayer at lunch, a gratitude moment before bed. These aren't rules; they're anchors. Let your rhythm and routines feel like a homecoming, not a hustle.

☐ **E: Embrace Progress Over Perfection:** You won't always feel "on fire" spiritually. And that's okay. God honors your consistency more than your intensity. Celebrate each moment you chose Him, each whisper of prayer, each pause for peace. Extend gratitude every evening as you remember His faithfulness.

End your day with thanks. List three things or steps you've taken, no matter how small, that you can be grateful for. Gratitude turns the soil of your soul and helps new growth take root. Over time, every small act waters your soul and leads to deep spiritual renewal.

Reflection Questions

1. When was the last time I felt truly connected to God?
2. What helped me feel close to Him in that season?

3. What's one area of my spiritual life I want to revive or rebuild?
4. Which of the three pillars (Prayer, Scripture, or Service) needs more intentional focus right now?
5. What "small act" of service can I offer this week from a heart of worship, not performance?
6. Where might God be inviting me to experience His presence in the middle of my everyday mess?
7. What is one small habit I can begin today to reconnect with God?
8. Where have I felt spiritually dry, and what may be contributing to it?
9. What gifts or acts of service feel natural and joyful to me?
10. How do I want to grow spiritually in this season of life?

A Prayer for Spiritual Renewal and Reconnection

Heavenly Father,

Thank You for loving me right here, right now, not because I have it all together, but because I am Yours. You see me fully every burden I carry, every place I feel weary or dry, and still, You choose to draw near. Even in the seasons when I've been too busy, too broken, or too distracted to come close, You've never left my side.

Today, I return to You not with perfection, but with my whole heart. I come not to perform but to be with You. Teach me to build my life on the unshakable foundation of Your truth, grace, and presence. Help me to pray with honesty, to listen with faith, and to rest in the promises of Your Word.

Water the soil of my soul again. Fill the dry places with Your living water. Reignite the fire in me to walk closely with You, not out of duty, but because I long for intimacy with my Father. Restore my joy. Anchor me in peace. Let my heart reflect Your goodness and my life reflect Your glory.

Teach me to serve not from an empty place, but from a heart overflowing with Your love. Quiet the noise, remove the pressure, and renew my mind. Awaken my soul. Help me see that this moment right here is purposeful and holy because You are in it.

I surrender again today. Thank You for being my strength, my rest, my source, and my ever-present help.

In Jesus' name, Amen.

GRACE CHECK-IN WORKSHEET

Use this GRACE Check-In Worksheet to nurture your spiritual foundation. This tool is designed to help you pause, reflect, and realign with God's presence throughout your day.

G – Ground Yourself
1. Take a moment to pause and check in with your spirit.
2. How are you really doing?
3. Response:

R – **Reflect on Your Current Reality**
1. Speak openly and honestly with God about your feelings, worries, or wins.
2. Response:

A – Act and Ask Boldly
1. Ask God for what you need today: peace, wisdom, healing, energy, clarity.
2. Response:

C – **Create Consistent Systems**
1. Read a scripture passage regularly and write one verse that speaks to you.
2. What is God saying?
3. Response:

E – **Embrace Progress Over Perfection**
1. Write down 3 things you are grateful for today, no matter how small.
2. Response:

In the next chapter, we'll explore how to pursue your personal goals with clarity and purpose, rooted in grace rather than pressure.

CHAPTER 9

Personal Goals: Pursuing What Lights You Up

Personal Goals That Honor God and Fulfill You

"Delight yourself in the Lord, and He will give you the desires of your heart."
— *Psalm 37:4, NIV*

Lisa sat in her car after dropping the kids off at school, staring at her color-coded planner filled with everyone else's priorities. Soccer practice. Work meetings. Doctor appointments. Church and community responsibilities. Her life looked full, but inside, she felt painfully empty. "I can't remember the last time I did something just because I wanted to," she whispered. "I don't even know what I want anymore."

If you've ever been in that place, I want you to know: you are not alone. And more importantly, you are not selfish for having dreams of your own. You were created for more than survival. You were made for overflow. You are a vessel of purpose, not just for everyone else's needs but for the beautiful desires God planted inside of you.

God-Sized Dreams Aren't Selfish; They're Purposeful

As women, especially those of us walking out roles as wives, moms, nurturers, business owners, and leaders, we tend to sacrifice our own dreams on the altar of service. We love deeply. We give completely. We carry homes, businesses, ministries, schedules, and emotions like champions, yet often silently grieve the dreams we shelved for another time. Somewhere along the way, we forget that we can't pour from an empty cup. Moreover, we often forget that God has placed those desires within us intentionally.

So let me ask you a personal question: What has God placed in your heart lately? Writing a book? Running a 5K? Learning a new language?

Launching a business? Going back to school? Picking up a paintbrush again? Putting yourself back on your list?

Those desires aren't distractions. They are often divine. They are invitations from God to step into a deeper expression of who you were always meant to be. The goal isn't to chase goals that impress the world. It's to pursue goals that align your heart with God's best for your life.

Why Traditional Goal Setting Falls Short for Women of Faith

SMART goals (Specific, Measurable, Achievable, Relevant, and Time-bound), though effective for some people, can feel sterile and disconnected from your spiritual walk. What if there were an improved way to set spirit-led goals that honor your season, your soul, and your Creator?

The SACRED Framework for Goal Setting:

S - Spirit-led: Rooted in prayer and aligned with God's character

A - Authentic: Reflecting your true identity, not cultural pressure

C - Compelling: Life-giving and energizing, not exhausting

R - Relational: Enhancing your connections, not isolating you

E - Evolutionary: Flexible and able to grow with your season

D - Dependent: Requiring God's strength more than your hustle

Discovering What Truly Matters

Before setting goals, pause and ask:
- What makes your heart come alive?
- What would you pursue if fear or failure weren't holding you back?

- What breaks your heart or stirs your soul?
- What have you always dreamed of doing but labeled as *"not now"* or *"not for someone like me"*?

Take time to really reflect on what breaks your heart and what stirs your soul. These are often divine clues pointing you toward your calling. Then look at your core values. Check off your top five from this list:

- ☐ Faith
- ☐ Family
- ☐ Freedom
- ☐ Growth
- ☐ Peace
- ☐ Service
- ☐ Legacy
- ☐ Health
- ☐ Creativity

Now ask yourself: "Are my current goals aligned with these values? Or am I living in tension with what matters most to me?"

Types of Life-Giving Goals

1. **Growth Goals:** These help you become more of who God created you to be.

- Learn a new skill.
- Take a course or earn a certification.
- Attend a spiritual retreat.
- Consider starting therapy or working with a coach.

2. **Contribution Goals:** These use your gifts to serve and uplift others.

- Start a blog, podcast, or support group.
- Mentor someone.
- Volunteer in your community.
- Create a product or service that solves a real problem.

3. **Experience Goals:** These infuse your life with joy, creativity, and a sense of presence.

- Take a meaningful trip.
- Learn to play an instrument or dance.
- Plan fun traditions with your children.
- Say yes to an adventure, just for the joy of it.

4. **Legacy Goals:** These are initiatives that build something lasting beyond your lifetime.

- Write a book.
- Launch a ministry.
- Start a nonprofit or scholarship fund.
- Pass down family values and stories through intentional traditions.

The 90-Day Goal Sprint

Instead of overwhelming yourself with long-term resolutions, break your dreams into focused 90-day sprints:

☐ Days 1–30: **Lay the foundation.** Pray. Build routines and support. Invite accountability.

☐ Days 31–60: **Build momentum.** Track progress. Celebrate small wins.

☐ Days 61–90: **Focus and press in.** Refine. Finish strong. Praise God for the growth. Celebrate.

Overcoming Self-Sabotage

Self-sabotage often wears a convincing disguise as busyness, guilt, fear, or perfectionism. However, underneath it all is a deep resistance to the woman you're becoming. The enemy knows that if he can't destroy you, he'll try to distract you, discourage you, or overwhelmingly fill your schedule and calendar with events and duties that have nothing to do with your purpose.

But you were not created to live stuck in cycles of busyness, hesitation or self-doubt. Romans 8:1 reminds us, "There is now no condemnation for those who are in Christ Jesus." That includes the voice that tells you don't have time, you're not enough, or that your dreams are too much.

To break free, start small: commit just 10 minutes a day to your goal. Replace lies with truth: you are not selfish for growing and you're being a good steward of God's gifts.

Expect failure to teach you, not define you. And when the fear of others' opinions rises, choose obedience over approval. Your future isn't waiting for perfection. It's waiting for permission, and that permission starts with you.

Examples of overcoming self-sabotage:

- "I don't have time." → You do. Start small, start with 10 minutes a day.
- "I feel selfish." → You aren't. Stewardship isn't selfish.
- "I might fail." → You might. But failure is a tutor, not a tombstone.
- "What will people think?" → That's not your burden or concern. Obedience is.

Create a Goal Support System

You were never meant to carry your dreams alone. Even Jesus chose twelve disciples to walk alongside Him because community isn't a luxury, it's a lifeline. Ecclesiastes 4:9–10 reminds us, "Two are better than one... If either of them falls down, one can help the other up."

The same is true for your personal goals and spiritual growth. A strong support system not only helps you stay focused but also breathes life into your journey when motivation fades.

Start by identifying one or two people who can walk with you in this season. Look for a prayer partner who will lift your dreams to God, a mentor who brings wisdom and perspective, a cheerleader who celebrates your steps (even the small ones), and an accountability friend or spouse who shares your values and helps you stay on track.

Don't wait for the perfect support circle; start building it, one meaningful connection at a time. And remember: where two or more are gathered in His name, God is right in the middle of it (Matthew 18:20).

Biblical Sisterhood: The Power of Support Systems

Throughout Scripture, we see that when women pursued divine purpose, they rarely did it alone. Mary, the mother of Jesus, immediately sought out Elizabeth after the angel's announcement, because carrying a promise often requires the comfort of someone who understands.

Ruth clung to Naomi, choosing mentorship and loyalty even in grief, which ultimately led her to divine provision and legacy. Esther leaned on the wisdom of Mordecai and the prayers of her community before stepping into the palace for such a time as this.

Even the women who discovered the empty tomb of Jesus went together. They were faith-filled women witnessing resurrection in community. These stories remind us that destiny is often walked out hand in hand. You don't need to be strong all the time. You just need to be surrounded. Your purpose is personal, but it was never meant to be walked out alone.

You don't have to do this alone. Surround yourself with:

- ☐ A prayer partner who lifts you up and speaks life
- ☐ A wise mentor who offers perspective and guidance
- ☐ A cheerleader who celebrates your steps
- ☐ A supportive spouse or accountability friend who shares your vision

Goal-Setting Is Spiritual

Sis, goal-setting isn't just about checklists or achievement. It can be a very sacred time between you and God. Every time you say "yes" to a God-aligned dream, no matter how small, it's an act of faith, a declaration that you still believe God has more in store for you.

For women like you who are juggling so much: womanhood, motherhood, marriage, career, caregiving, healing from betrayal, or rebuilding after burnout. Goal-setting can feel like a luxury. However, it's actually a critical lifeline. When you align your goals with heaven's heartbeat, you're not chasing empty success; you're walking in divine assignment.

God isn't asking you to strive harder. He's inviting you to partner with Him. You were created in His image (Genesis 1:27), which means you carry within you the power to co-create, to build, to nurture, and to multiply. Whether your dream is to write a book, go back to school, open a business, or simply find joy again after a season of loss. When that desire is rooted in Him, it's no longer just a personal goal. It becomes a spiritual calling.

You're not just setting goals. You're prophesying over your future. You're modeling courage and faith to your children, your community, and younger women still finding their voice. You're reminding your soul that it's never too late for God to move. The same God who split the sea, opened wombs, and raised the dead is still in the business of breakthroughs; and He wants to do something miraculous through you.

You don't have to hustle or prove your worth. You simply have to believe that the God who gave you the dream will also equip you to see it through. Every step you take is not just progress; it's worship.

So dream boldly. Move forward prayerfully. And remember: you don't just accomplish something. Every time you embark upon achieving a goal, you become someone. A woman fully alive in her purpose, rooted in faith, and unstoppable with God by her side.

Affirmation Practice:

- ✓ I am allowed to grow.
- ✓ I am worthy of joy.
- ✓ I am walking in purpose.
- ✓ I am becoming all God created me to be.

Empowerment Thought

You are no longer the woman you were 90 days ago. You've grown wiser in your decisions, stronger in your spirit, and more beautifully aligned with who God created you to be. Keep pressing forward. Keep dreaming boldly. Keep inviting God into every step. You're not behind. You're right on time. And those dreams stirring in your heart? They're not too big; they're precisely the right size for the God who gave them to you.

Applying the GRACE Method to Your Personal Goals

G: Ground Yourself in God's Truth: Before you chase any goal, anchor yourself in God's promises. You are not selfish for having dreams; you are stewarding the life God gave you.

Delight yourself in the Lord, and He will give you the desires of your heart.
—Psalm 37:4, NIV

For I know the plans I have for you,' declares the Lord, 'plans to prosper you and not to harm you, plans to give you hope and a future. —Jeremiah 29:11, NIV

Let these truths quiet your doubts: God delights in your delight. He wants you to dream with Him.

R: Reflect on Your Current Reality: What season are you in right now? What do you long for? What feels missing? Take a gentle but honest look at your life: Are your goals aligned with your current responsibilities, energy, and values? Or are they draining you or disconnected from what matters most?

Write down:

- What's working?
- What's draining me?
- What dream keeps resurfacing in my heart?

A: Act with Intentional Steps: Choose one God-honoring goal that excites your spirit, no matter how small. Converse with God honestly about your fears, hopes, and next steps. Create a *90-day goal sprint.* Break it into bite-sized actions. Just 10–15 minutes a day is enough to begin. Progress doesn't require perfection; it just requires one to start.

Try:

1. Creating a goal journal or vision board.
2. Scheduling your goal time like an appointment with God.
3. Taking one bold step this week (e.g., signing up, reaching out, preparing your space).

C: Create Consistent Systems: Consistency creates change. Set small weekly check-ins to track your progress and course-correct without shame. Stack your goal time with habits that already exist (e.g., pray before you plan, listen to a podcast during laundry, review your goals every Sunday evening). Grace-based systems make success sustainable.

Ask:

- What time of day works best for me to take action?
- Where do I need to simplify, delegate, or set boundaries to create space?

E: Embrace Progress Over Perfection: You don't have to do it all at once. You just have to keep saying yes. Every effort, no matter how small, is worship when done in faith. Celebrate your obedience, not just your outcomes. Miracles unfold through daily faithfulness. So, thank God for the clarity, courage, and capacity to dream, and for every small step forward each day.

Reflect and affirm:

- "God, thank You for the strength to try again."
- "I'm not who I was 90 days ago."
- "My progress matters, even when it's messy."

Reflection Questions:

1. What dreams have I shelved that God might be inviting me to revisit?
2. Which core values matter most to me right now?
3. What small step can I take today toward a SACRED goal?

A Prayer for Purpose-Driven Goals

Heavenly Father,

Thank You for planting purpose in my heart. Thank You for reminding me that I was made for more than survival. Help me to dream again, not for selfish ambition, but to glorify You in all that I pursue. Align my desires with Your will. Give me courage to step out, grace to keep going, and wisdom to discern what matters most. Let my goals reflect Your beauty, and my life be a testimony of Your faithfulness.

In Jesus' name, Amen.

Coming Up Next: Let's discuss ways to strengthen your marriage and personal relationships while pursuing your dreams. You can love your people and love yourself, too. Let's explore how.

CHAPTER 10

Marriage: Love on Purpose

Building a Marriage That Thrives Through Every Season

Though one may be overpowered, two can defend themselves. A cord of three strands is not quickly broken. — Ecclesiastes 4:12, NIV.

Marriage isn't always easy, but it is redeemable. When even one heart is willing to stay soft, pray boldly, and love with intention, God can begin the work of restoration. And when both partners invite Him in, anchoring the marriage in love, prayer, and daily intention, what once felt broken can become more beautiful than ever imagined.

Scripture reminds us that "with God all things are possible" (Matthew 19:26, NIV), and that includes healing what's been hurt, rebuilding what's been shaken, and renewing a love story that reflects His grace. A marriage anchored in prayer, humility, and perseverance can become not just a testimony but a miracle in motion.

Whether you're just newly stepping into this covenant or you've walked through decades of "for better or worse," one truth remains: marriage is far more than emotional companionship. It's a divine calling, a sacred covenant, a solemn agreement or promise between God and humans that establishes a relationship with specific commitments and obligations.

It signifies a permanent union, not easily dissolved, with vows of faithfulness and mutual support. It is a daily decision to love with grace, to forgive as you have been forgiven, to lead with humility, and to partner with God in building something that lasts beyond this life.

Spiritually speaking, the enemy doesn't fight or waste his energy on what doesn't matter. He targets marriage because it matters deeply to you, to your legacy, and to the heart of God. Marriage is generational soil. It's where faith is planted, where stability is formed, and where future families are shaped. It's kingdom-building work at its most personal level. So let's choose to build and protect your marriage with fierce intention, unwavering faith, and purpose.

Marriage is a Sacred Partnership

Above all, love each other deeply, because love covers over a multitude of sins.
— *1 Peter 4:8, NIV*

In Scripture, the covenant of marriage is more than a contract; it is a sacred, binding promise made before God, marked by faithfulness, sacrifice, and lasting commitment. It's not meant to be left broken when things get hard, but to be upheld with reverence, even when the journey is challenging.

Biblical marriage is a holy union designed to reflect God's unwavering love for His people. It involves specific vows, faithfulness, honor, mutual service, and calls both husband and wife to walk in humility, forgiveness, and grace. This covenant is not merely about surviving together but about partnering with God to build something eternal: a relationship that bears witness to His goodness, leaves a legacy of love, and models His truth for future generations.

Marriage isn't just about staying together. It's about growing together. It's about forgiving often, choosing humility, and speaking life when silence feels easier. It's about bearing one another's burdens and cheering one another on. When two people are aligned with God and each other, their union becomes a force the world cannot shake.

What Does a Thriving Marriage Really Mean?

For many women, marriage has not always lived up to the dream they envisioned. It has included unexpected disappointments, sickness, long seasons of silence, betrayal, or daily moments that felt more like survival than partnership. But here's the good news: God does not waste anything, not even the broken pieces of a hurting marriage. He is the God of restoration, and He delights in making all things new, including your relationship.

Take a deep breath. You are not alone in this journey. Whether you're newly married or decades in, it's essential to pause and ask yourself: What does success in my marriage really mean to me? Is it simply getting along? Is it the feeling of being seen, cherished, and safe? Is it spiritual intimacy, laughter, or dreaming together again?

Success in marriage doesn't look like perfection. It sounds like a prayer whispered in the midst of an argument. It's choosing forgiveness over bitterness or resentment. It's holding hands through uncertainty and staying when walking away would feel easier. It's showing up again with love, humility, and grace.

Let go of society's version of "marriage goals" and embrace God's version of growth. True success in marriage is two imperfect people choosing to reflect the covenant of Christ's love daily. Not by performance, but by presence. Not by flawless execution, but by faithful intention.

Coaching Reflection: Define Your Shared Vision

Don't underestimate the power of vision in marriage. Without it, couples drift. With it, they build. Set aside time to ask yourself, and eventually your spouse, what love looks like in action within your home. Is it daily encouragement? Laughter? Shared goals? Peace? Purpose?

Write it down. Speak it aloud. Revisit it when things feel heavy. Your vision becomes your compass.

If you're walking this path alone right now, start by writing a vision for how you desire your marriage to be and how you want to show up as a wife. Invite God into that vision, and trust that He can move in your spouse's heart even when you cannot.

Evaluate Honestly, Love Intentionally

Healing starts with honesty, not blame. Ask yourself: Where is my marriage thriving? Where is it hurting? Do I feel valued, seen, and heard? Does my spouse? Then, take gentle, grace-filled action.

Start small:

- ☐ Pray together (even 30 seconds matters and makes a difference).
- ☐ Hold hands again, even if it feels awkward at first.
- ☐ Leave a kind note in their car or send a Scripture text during the day.
- ☐ Celebrate your spouse publicly.
- ☐ Choose kind, intentional words that touch the heart.
- ☐ Ask, "What do you need from me this week?", don't view it as a burden, but as an act of love.

These small shifts soften hearts and restore emotional safety.

Appreciation, Gratitude, and Communication

Let everything you do be done in love {motivated and inspired by God's love for us}.
— *1 Corinthians 16:14, AMP*

Marriage thrives when we speak life. Gratitude is not just a feeling; it's a spiritual practice. List the things you appreciate about your spouse: their kindness, their quirks, their effort, their presence. Then, tell them. Brag about them to your children. Speak well of them to others. Let your words be water, not weeds, in the garden of your relationship. And when communication feels difficult, lead with humility and truth.

Try:

- "I felt loved when you…"
- "I'm thankful for how you handled…"
- "I know we're both tired, but I want to stay close."

Words shape atmospheres. Let yours build rather than break.

Support, Sacrifice, and Shared Dreams

Marriage isn't about keeping score. It's about lifting each other up. Ask yourself: What excites my spouse right now? Am I making space for their dreams, too, or have we become only roommates managing a to-do list?

Bring back the art of dreaming together. One beautiful practice is a "Vision Walk." Once a month, go for a walk with no phones, no agenda, just prayer, conversation, and dreaming about the future. Ask God: What are You calling us to build together?

Intimacy, Joy, and Everyday Romance

Don't wait for special occasions to connect. Intimacy starts in the little things:

- Dance in the kitchen.
- Laugh at old photos.
- Hug longer.
- Sit close.
- Say "I love you" and mean it.

True joy in marriage comes from finding delight and satisfaction in one another within the safety of a long-term, God-honoring covenant. Scripture reminds us that lasting fulfillment is not found outside the marriage bond but nurtured within it.

A husband is called to cherish and remain faithful to his wife, and a wife is called to do the same for her husband. The success of this sacred union is dependent on the condition of each spouse's heart, how connected they choose to be with God, and how intentional they are in choosing each other, every single day.

Romance isn't dead, and it doesn't have to disappear with time; it simply requires attention. Like anything worth keeping alive, it must be fed regularly with laughter, affection, kindness, and presence. So, keep it light. Keep it fun. Keep it real. And watch your love deepen in the most beautiful ways.

Rejoice in the wife of your youth. — *Proverbs 5:18, NIV.*

Forgiveness, Grace, and Emotional Safety

Two imperfect people. One holy promise. That's marriage. If you've been holding pain, anger, or silent resentment, bring it to God. Then bring it to your spouse when the time is right. Healing words open the door to intimacy:

- "I was wrong."
- "I'm sorry."
- "I want to do better."
- "Can we start fresh?"

Emotional safety is the soil where connection grows. Let grace be the language of your home.

Be completely humble and gentle; be patient, bearing with one another in love.
— *Ephesians 4:2, NIV.*

Presence, Reflection, and Daily Touchpoints

You don't need hours. You need intention.
- Try a 15-minute evening check-in:
- "How are you? Really?" Or a midday "thinking of you" text.

Presence builds trust, even in busy seasons.

Nightly Practice:
- Reflect: How did I love well today?
- Renew: What can I do differently tomorrow?

Legacy, Long-Term Vision, and the Choices We Make Today

Marriage is more than a commitment between two people; it's a living legacy, a deeply spiritual story that outlives your daily routines and disagreements. It's a testimony unfolding in real time. The way you love your spouse today has a lasting impact on more than just the atmosphere of your home. It ripples into your children's sense of safety, your community's understanding of faithfulness, and your own future reflection.

I say this not from theory, but from experience. I almost lost my husband, more than once, to strokes that came without warning. One day, we were going through the day as ususal. The next, I was in a hospital room, praying through beeping monitors and uncertain diagnoses. In those moments, everything changed, and none of the real, challenging marital problems *or* petty issues mattered.

What rose to the surface of what did matter were the little things I had missed so deeply about the man I married: his laughter, his voice, the way he played and joked with our children, and his steady presence throughout our long days. Facing a life or death situation, changes your perspective.

If your spouse weren't here tomorrow, what would you ache for most? Their smile or laughter? The way they reach for your hand without thinking? The sound of their footsteps walking through the front door? Those everyday moments are the real treasure. Don't wait for a crisis to make you see it. Prayerfully, it won't take a life or death situation for your spouse to see it either.

The truth is, life changes fast. One unexpected phone call, one diagnosis, one accident, and everything shifts. And while we can't control every circumstance, we can choose to love with urgency, to extend grace more quickly, to hug longer, laugh louder, and forgive faster.

You don't need a perfect marriage to leave a powerful legacy. You need daily decisions grounded in kindness, honesty, presence, and joy. These are the bricks legacy is built on, laid one small act of love at a time. Don't wait. Start doing it today.

So today, choose to remember what matters most. Look into the eyes of the one God gave you and ask yourself, What will I be glad I did more of if tomorrow never comes? Then go do that. Love with intention. Speak with tenderness. And live in such a way that even your arguments leave room for mercy.

Your marriage, whether flourishing, fragile, damaged, or somewhere in between, is worth fighting for and protecting. Even in its imperfections, even through the cracks, God can bring beauty. Your legacy isn't written in perfection; it's written in the quiet acts of faithfulness: through whispered prayers, unseen tears, shared laughter, and the courageous choice to stay and keep choosing each other. Every moment you choose grace over giving up, you are allowing God to restore, renew, and redeem what He Himself has joined together and blessed.

Final Empowerment Thought

Marriage doesn't thrive on grand gestures. It thrives on God's grace, love and mercy, spoken, lived, and renewed every single day. It thrives when you show up even when it's hard, stay soft and loving even when you're hurt, and keep choosing each other when the world tells you not to bother.

God sees your heart. He knows your longing. Ask Him for direction and guidance. He is with you as you build, heal, or begin again. So, breathe. Forgive. Laugh. Touch. Pray. Let your marriage become a living testimony, not of perfection, but of persistence, not of flawlessness, but of faith. The best chapters may still be ahead.

Your marriage matters. You matter. And with God, restoration is not only possible; it's promised.

Encouraging Scriptures for Restoration & Reconciliation in Marriage

1. God Can Restore What Was Lost:

I will repay you for the years the locusts have eaten... You will have plenty to eat, until you are full, and you will praise the name of the Lord your God, who has worked wonders for you. —Joel 2:25-26, NIV

This verse reminds couples that no matter how much time has been lost to pain or conflict, God can restore.

2. God Woos Us Back to Love

But then I will win her back once again. I will lead her into the desert and speak tenderly to her... She will give herself to me there, as she did long ago when she was young. —Hosea 2:14-15, NLT

This is a powerful image of God pursuing a broken relationship, symbolic of marital restoration.

3. Love Covers a Multitude of Sins

Above all, love each other deeply, because love covers over a multitude of sins. —1 Peter 4:8, NIV

This encourages couples to love beyond offense, with forgiveness and depth.

4. God Is Doing a New Thing

See, I am doing a new thing! Now it springs up; do you not perceive it? —Isaiah 43:19, NIV

This is a reminder that even in the wilderness of marriage, God can bring forth something new and life-giving.

5. Ministry of Reconciliation

All this is from God, who reconciled us to himself through Christ and gave us the ministry of reconciliation. —*2 Corinthians 5:18, NIV*

Marriage restoration mirrors the gospel's work of reconciliation.

6. Be Kind & Forgive

Be kind and compassionate to one another, forgiving each other, just as in Christ God forgave you. —*Ephesians 4:32, NIV*

Forgiveness is the soil where restoration grows.

7. A Cord of Three Strands

Though one may be overpowered, two can defend themselves. A cord of three strands is not quickly broken. —*Ecclesiastes 4:9-12, NIV*

A reminder that marriage with God at the center is not easily destroyed.

Applying the GRACE Method to Your Marriage

Marriage must be a rhythm of love, not perfection. Because the strength of your marriage isn't built on flawless days, but on faithful ones. The GRACE Method offers you a path to reconnect, renew, and rebuild one prayerful step at a time.

☐ **G: Ground Yourself in God's Truth:** Marriage is God's idea, not man's invention. He is deeply invested in your union and stands with you, even in the hardest moments. You are not doing this alone. He is the third strand in your cord, your anchor when emotions shift and storms come.

Though one may be overpowered, two can defend themselves. A cord of three strands is not quickly broken. — *Ecclesiastes 4:12, NIV*

Therefore what God has joined together, let no one separate. — *Mark 10:9, NIV*

When you root your expectations in God's promises, you're no longer building on shaky ground, but on the solid rock of His truth and presence.

☐ **R: Reflect on Your Current Reality:** Take a deep breath and be honest, again without shame or judgment.

- Where is your marriage flourishing?
- Where is it feeling dry or disconnected?
- Are you in a season of newlywed joy, parenting chaos, emotional rebuilding, or rediscovery?

Ask God to gently reveal what needs healing, and what needs nourishing. Reflection is not about blame; it's about clarity, compassion, and invitation.

☐ **A: Act with Intentional Steps:** Small, intentional actions can transform the atmosphere of your home. Choose one area to nurture this week: prayer, kindness, affection, appreciation, or communication. Don't underestimate what a 5-minute check-in, a handwritten note, or a walk together can do.

Connection doesn't require perfection; it requires pursuit. Choose love in motion.

☐ **C: Create Consistent Systems:** Love needs a rhythm to stay alive. Set aside one intentional time each week to truly reconnect. Whether it's a quiet coffee, a purpose-filled "marriage meeting," a date night, or Sunday evening prayer. Let these moments become sacred rituals that build trust and unity over time.

Systems sustain intimacy when life gets busy. When it's built into your week, you won't have to chase connection; it will already have a place.

☐ **E: Embrace Progress Over Perfection:** Your goal is not to have a perfect marriage; it's to have a growing one. Celebrate every step, every effort, and every restart, not just the major milestones. Give grace freely to your spouse, and especially to yourself. Love isn't about flawless performance. It's about daily devotion.

Every kind word, every effort to reconnect, every prayer whispered for your marriage is seed planted in holy, consecrated ground. Don't wait for a dramatic turnaround. Praise God for every bit of progress. Choose to show up again tomorrow. And the next day. And the one after that.

Let this GRACE rhythm guide your heart and your home. With God at the center, every marriage has hope, and every effort you make can bear beautiful fruit.

Reflection Questions:

1. What season is my marriage in right now?
2. How can I show love to my spouse in a way that feels meaningful to them?
3. What have I been holding back that needs to be shared in a gentle and truthful manner?
4. Where do I need to give more grace?
5. How can I invite God more deeply into our relationship?
6. What daily habit can help us stay emotionally connected?
7. What is one small action I can take this week to strengthen our connection?

A Powerful Prayer for Your Marriage

Heavenly Father,

Thank You for the beautiful gift of the covenant of marriage. Thank You for the love we share, the lessons we've learned, and even the hard places that have stretched and refined us. Lord, help me to see my spouse through Your eyes, with compassion when it's hard, with grace when I feel weary, and with patience that mirrors Your heart.

When distance grows between us, give us the courage to close the gap. When communication breaks down, teach us to listen, not just to words, but to each other's hearts. When resentment, bitterness, or misunderstanding creeps in, flood those spaces with Your peace, love, and forgiveness.

God, breathe new life into the tired parts of our marriage. Rekindle joy where it's gone dim. Restore laughter, warmth, and connection. Let our marriage reflect Your love, a love that sacrifices, endures, and heals. Help us to grow not just older together, but closer, closer to one another, and closer to You.

When moving forward feels impossible, remind us that nothing is too hard or broken for You to restore. You are the God of resurrection power. Help us to lay every piece of our marriage: our arguments, our personalities, our parenting, our past, and our dreams on Your throne and leave it there in trust.

Make our home a sanctuary where Your Spirit dwells, where grace flows freely, where we speak life and choose one another daily. Remind us that we are not alone in this covenant; that You are always the third strand in our cord, the anchor when we're drifting, and the glue when things fall apart.

Strengthen us where we are tired. Heal what's been wounded. Restore what's been lost. And above all, help our marriage to be a living testimony of Your faithfulness, Your mercy, and Your ability to make all things new.

We trust You with our whole hearts, our home, and our future.

In Jesus' name, Amen.

Coming Up Next: In our next chapter, we'll explore the purpose-filled calling and the practical tools of parenting with love, grace, and leadership. You can lead your children well, and still care for your soul.

CHAPTER 11

Family: Building a Legacy of Love

Building a Legacy of Love

But as for me and my household, we will serve the Lord. —Joshua 24:15, NIV

One summer afternoon, I was juggling a dozen things at once: laundry piled high, chores unfinished, and a pineapple upside-down cake in the oven for my family. When the timer beeped, I pulled the cake out, flipped it onto the platter to cool, and something about it seemed… off. But I didn't have time to figure it out. I was already off to the laundry room, gathering what felt like my sixth load of the day to fold.

Hours later, when it was time to serve dessert, I finally discovered the issue; my family's confused, polite smiles gave it away before anyone said a word. I had forgotten the sugar. In all my multitasking, I had baked an entire cake without one of the most essential ingredients.

Standing there still in my pajamas, flour still all over me and probably in my hair too, tears beginning to rise with frustration, I felt like a complete failure. But in that moment, God gave me a quiet revelation: my family didn't need a Pinterest-perfect memory; they needed me. Present, real, available, and loving. Even when things went wrong.

I scraped the unsweetened cake into the trash and tossed a store-bought cookie onto each plate instead. But instead of disappointment, laughter erupted. My kids turned my baking blunder into a running joke. That "failed" dessert became one of our most cherished memories.

And that's what family is all about. Not perfection, but presence. Not flawless execution, but faithful love. Your family doesn't need a perfect you; they need a present you. This is your first ministry. It's the sacred space where love takes root, character is shaped, faith is formed, and legacy begins.

The HEART Method for Building Family Legacy

Let's explore a framework that brings intention, grace, and joy back into your home life. We'll call it **the HEART Method:**

H – Honor Each Person's Unique Design

E – Establish Non-Negotiable Values

A – Activate Daily Connection Rituals

R – Respond with Grace When Things Break

T – Transform Ordinary Moments into Sacred Memories

Let's dive deeper into each component of this framework.

H – Honor Each Person's Unique Design

Each family member is a masterpiece, handcrafted by God. That strong-willed child? They might be a leader in training. The quiet one? A deep thinker with compassion beyond their years. Your spouse? Created with strengths that complement your own.

Take time to notice how God designed each person in your family:

- What are their strengths?
- What makes them light up?
- What do they need more of: attention, freedom, words of affirmation?

When you see your family through God's eyes, you create an environment of affirmation, not comparison. That alone can shift your home from chaos to calm.

I praise You because I am fearfully and wonderfully made. — Psalm 139:14, NIV

E – Establish Non-Negotiable Values

Your family culture is being built either by design or by default. Craft a mission statement that accurately reflects your core values. It doesn't have to be fancy, just heartfelt and true.

Here's how:

1. Gather the family (kids included!)
2. Ask: "What matters most to us?" "How do we want people to feel in our home?"
3. Write a statement in clear, simple language.
4. Post it where you'll see it daily.

Example:

"We choose faith over fear. We speak life. We forgive quickly. We serve joyfully. We love like Jesus."

This becomes your family's "why." When life gets hectic or hard, you return to it.

Train up a child in the way he should go, and when he is old, he will not depart from it. — Proverbs 22:6, KJV

A – Activate Daily Connection Rituals

Love grows in the little things. You don't need elaborate activities, just meaningful rhythms that make your family feel seen and safe.

Try these **"Daily 3"** check-ins:

1. Morning moment: Hug, blessing, prayer, or a kind word before everyone scatters
2. Midday touchpoint: A quick "thinking of you" text or voice note
3. Evening reflection: Ask, "What was your high and low today?"

I used to think connection required a big production. Now I know: folding laundry side by side, laughing in the carpool lane, or cooking dinner together can build unbreakable bonds.

R – Respond with Grace When Things Break

There will be challenging moments. Misunderstandings. Raised voices. Doors closed. Distance formed. But grace is the glue that holds us together.

When it falls apart:

- Pause. Breathe.
- Say: "I was wrong. I'm sorry."
- Ask: "Can we try again?"
- Invite God in: "Lord, help us heal what's been hurt."

Be completely humble and gentle; be patient, bearing with one another in love.
— *Ephesians 4:2, NIV*

Every family has moments of rupture, but grace creates moments of repair.

T – Transform the Ordinary into Sacred

The most powerful memories won't be the expensive vacations. They'll be the traditions, the inside jokes, the nightly prayers, and the rituals no one ever planned but everyone remembers.

Ideas:

- *Family Fun Jar:* Fill it with low-cost ideas, such as a dance party, park picnic, or storytelling night.
- *"Yes" Day:* Let your child make all the decisions (within reason!)
- *Prayer Walks:* Walk the neighborhood and pray over neighbors, schools, and dreams

Legacy is formed in repetition. What you do again and again becomes what your family carries forward.

Let all that you do be done in love. — *1 Corinthians 16:14, AMP*

Family Legacy Reflection Questions

1. What makes our family unique?
2. What values are we modeling?

3. How am I intentionally showing up in love this week?
4. Where do I need to extend more grace, or ask for it?
5. What do I want my children to remember most about me?

Family Legacy Audit (Rate 1–5)

____Connection: Do we enjoy being together?

____Communication: Do we discuss tough topics with kindness & love?

____Tradition: Do we have routines that bring us joy?

____Spiritual Life: Are we growing in faith together?

____Fun Factor: Are we laughing, playing, and making memories?

Choose your lowest number. What's one change you can make this week?

When Your Family Feels Broken

Maybe your family is struggling. Maybe your story includes distance, addiction, betrayal, divorce, disappointment, or deep heartbreak that seems too tangled to mend, ever. If that's you, please lean in and hear this with all the love and hope I can offer: **God specializes in restoration.** He doesn't just fix what's broken, He rebuilds it stronger, deeper, and more beautiful than it was before.

He heals the brokenhearted and binds up their wounds. — Psalm 147:3, NIV

You are not disqualified from legacy because of pain. Your family isn't beyond repair because of what's happened. **Brokenness often becomes the very place where God does His most profound work.** He steps into fractured spaces and begins to knit hearts together in ways we couldn't have imagined.

The Lord is close to the brokenhearted and saves those who are crushed in spirit.
— Psalm 34:18, NIV

Let's look at some **biblical examples of families who faced devastation and witnessed divine restoration:**

Joseph's family: Betrayed by his own brothers, sold into slavery, and separated for years, Joseph had every reason to remain bitter. But through a process of healing, he forgave and was used by God to rescue the very family that once harmed him. (Genesis 50:20)

Hosea and Gomer: God called Hosea to love a wife who would be unfaithful, as a living picture of God's redemptive love for His people. Even when she walked away, Hosea pursued her, restored her, and welcomed her home. (Hosea 3:1)

The Prodigal Son: A son leaves home, wastes everything, and returns empty-handed. But instead of rejection, he's met with open arms, a robe, and a feast. That's the picture of a parent's heart, and God's heart, for restoration. (Luke 15:11–32)

These stories remind us that healing is possible, even after betrayal, loss, and years of silence. Restoration may not always look like a perfect, tied-up ending, but it always begins with hope, obedience, and prayerful action.

Coaching Encouragement:

1. **Start With Your Part:** You may not be able to control everything in your family dynamic, but you can control your response to it.

Ask yourself:

- "What's one small way I can show love or extend grace this week?"
- "What apology have I been avoiding that could create space for healing?"

2. **Pray Strategically, Not Just Emotionally:** Instead of just praying out of pain, pray with precision. Create a list of scriptures to pray over each family member.

Examples:

- For a child in rebellion: "All your children will be taught by the Lord, and great will be their peace." — Isaiah 54:13, NIV
- For a strained marriage: "Let love and faithfulness never leave you… write them on the tablet of your heart." — Proverbs 3:3, NIV

3. **Create a Safe Space for Reconnection:** Start small. Send a text. Write a letter. Leave a note. Sit down and simply ask, "How can I support you today?" Even if they don't respond as you hoped, keep showing up with kindness. Restoration is often a slow, steady process.

4. **Lean Into Counseling and Community:** Healing is hard work. Don't do it alone. Invite a trusted spiritual mentor, counselor, or small group into your journey. God often uses others to speak life, wisdom, and accountability into our broken spaces.

Scriptures to Stand On for Family Restoration

Study and meditate upon these Scriptures:

God places the lonely in families; he sets the prisoners free and gives them joy.
— Psalm 68:6, NLT

They will rebuild the ancient ruins and restore the places long devastated; they will renew the ruined cities that have been devastated for generations.
— Isaiah 61:4, NIV

Love bears all things, believes all things, hopes all things, endures all things. Love never fails. — 1 Corinthians 13:7–8, NKJV

A Prayer for Family Restoration

Heavenly Father,

You see the places in my family that feel broken beyond repair. You know the words that were said, the wounds that were never healed, and the silence that speaks louder than words. Lord, I surrender it all to You. I invite You into the pain, the fear, the regret, and the hope I still hold.

Where hearts have grown hard, soften them. Where communication has shut down, open a door. Where distance has settled in, create new pathways of closeness. Where trust has been shattered, begin the gentle rebuilding.

Help me to love with Your love: to forgive, to believe, to hope, and to endure. I choose to fight for my family, not with my fists, but on my knees. Let restoration begin with me. Let Your Spirit bring peace where there was tension, unity where there was division, and joy where sorrow has stayed too long.

In Jesus' name, Amen.

Final Encouragement: Your Family Legacy Starts Today

You don't have to be the perfect parent or partner. You just have to show up with love and intention. Even if you didn't come from a healed or healthy home, you can build one now. Even if your home feels messy or distant, God is still in the midst of it.

Your children won't remember every meal, but they'll remember your smile. They won't recall every word, but they'll remember how you made them feel. Keep sowing love, grace, and joy. Your legacy isn't in perfection; it's in presence.

Legacy Builder Challenge:

Today, choose one family member and honor them. Leave a note. Ask a deep question. Make their favorite snack. Speak a blessing over their life. These are the seeds that grow into generational impact.

Applying the GRACE Method to Your Family Life

Let the GRACE Method guide how you build your home, not with pressure, but with purpose:

☐ **G: Ground Yourself in God's Truth:** Your family is your first ministry. God handpicked you for this role, not because you're perfect, but because you're willing.

But as for me and my household, we will serve the Lord. —*Joshua 24:15, NIV*

☐ **R: Reflect on Your Current Reality:** What areas of your family life feel healthy, joyful, and connected? What areas feel strained, neglected, or chaotic? Take time to reflect with compassion and clarity, without shame.

☐ **A: Act with Intentional Steps:** Choose one area this week to nurture intentionally, whether that's listening better, planning a memory-making moment, affirming a family member, or simply showing up with presence. Small shifts lead to lasting change.

☐ **C: Create Consistent Systems:** Establish daily or weekly routines that foster connection, such as family dinners, bedtime prayers, Saturday morning walks, or tech-free evenings. These simple habits become heaven-kissed and Spirit-filled when practiced with love and care.

☐ **E: Embrace Progress Over Perfection:** You don't need to do everything right. You just need to show up with love and grace. Celebrate the moments of growth, laughter, and reconnection. Let your legacy be built on love, not perfection.

Reflection Questions

1. What do I want my family to remember most about our time together?
2. Where am I modeling love and grace well, and where can I grow?
3. What small, intentional habit can I introduce this week to create deeper connection in my home?
4. How can I help each family member feel seen, heard, and valued?
5. What does a legacy of faith, joy, and unity look like in our household?

A Powerful Prayer for Your Family

Heavenly Father,

Thank You for the beautiful gift of family. Thank You for every soul under my roof, every heartbeat that You've entrusted to my care. Lord, I confess that some days feel more like a struggle for survival than a divine legacy-building experience, but I know You are in the midst of it all.

Help me to see my family through Your eyes, with patience, with compassion, and with a renewed sense of purpose. Teach me to slow down and listen, to speak life, to forgive quickly, and to love deeply. Fill our home with Your presence, Your peace, and Your priorities.

Where there is brokenness, bring healing. Where there is distance, draw us closer. Where there is weariness, breathe new strength. Make our family a reflection of Your Kingdom, a safe place, a holy place, a place where love never gives up.

Let Your kingdom come and let Your will be done in our family and home life. Remind me, Lord, that my love doesn't have to be perfect to leave a lasting impact. Just faithful. Just present. Just rooted in You.

In Jesus' name, Amen.

LEGACY BUILDER CHALLENGE WORKSHEET: CREATING A FAMILY THAT REFLECTS GOD'S LOVE

Your family legacy is not built in a day, but it is shaped by the choices you make each day. This worksheet is your invitation to move from inspiration to action, one intentional choice at a time.

Step 1: Define Your Family Mission Statement

As a family (or on your own if needed), answer the questions below to help create your Family Mission Statement. Then write it out.

What do we want our family to be known for?
Example: Kindness, faith, forgiveness, laughter, service

_____

What values matter most in our home?

_____

How do we want people to feel when they enter our home?

_____

What kind of legacy do we want to leave behind?

_____

Your Family Mission Statement:
"The {Last Name} family exists to..."

_____

_____

Step 2: The Family Legacy Audit

Rate each area from 1 (Needs Major Growth) to 10 (Thriving):

Areas:
_____Connection
_____Communication
_____Traditions & Memories
_____Faith Formation
_____Fun & Joy
_____Emotional Safety
_____Support for Dreams
_____Respect & Grace in Conflict

Choose the area with the lowest score. What's one small thing you can do this week to improve it?

_____

Step 3: Activate the Daily 3

Use this checklist to build connection in your daily routines.

- ☐ **Morning Moment:** A hug, prayer, or loving word before the day starts
- ☐ **Midday Check-In:** A text, a lunch note, or a simple "thinking of you"
- ☐ **Evening Reflection:** Share the highs/lows of the day together

How did your family respond to the Daily 3 this week?

_____

Step 4: Celebrate a Family Member

Pick one person in your family to intentionally honor this week.

Name: _____

What do you appreciate about them?

_____

How will you show it? (Note, text, conversation, surprise, etc.)

_____

Step 5: Pray Over Your Family Together

Gather your family and read this prayer aloud, or modify it to fit your heart:

Lord,
We thank You for our home, our love, and our journey together. Teach us to honor each other, to forgive freely, and to build with joy. May our family reflect Your love, walk in Your truth, and be a light to the world. Help us create a legacy that glorifies You for generations to come.
In Jesus' name, Amen.

Bonus Challenge:

Pick one day this week for **a Legacy Day**: a special, simple activity with your family that helps build lasting memories.

- ☐ Family walk
- ☐ Backyard picnic
- ☐ Worship night
- ☐ Cooking together

☐ Gratitude jar
☐ "I love you because..." notes

Legacy Day Date: _____

CHAPTER 12

Parenting: Leading with Love and Structure

Leading with Love and Structure

Children are a heritage from the Lord, offspring a reward from Him.
— Psalm 127:3, NIV

Parenting is purpose-filled, stretching work. It's beautiful and exhausting, heart-expanding and heart-wrenching, all in the same breath. From the moment your child is placed in your arms (or your heart), you're invited into a divine assignment that grows and shapes both of you. And let me say this upfront: there is no such thing as a perfect parent. But there is such a thing as a prayerful, present, and purpose-driven one.

I recall a day when I was trying to do it all: making dinner, folding laundry, returning calls, and helping with math homework. In the middle of that chaos, my daughter asked if I could just sit and braid her hair while we watched her favorite movie. I almost said no. But something in me whispered, "This is a moment that matters." And you know what? That quiet time together ended up being the anchor in an otherwise stormy day for both of us.

Let's walk through **ten powerful ways to parent with love and intention**, not for perfection, but for legacy.

1. How Healthy Is Your Connection?

Before we discuss parenting strategies, let's pause to examine the heart of it all: connection. Do your children feel seen? Safe? Deeply loved? Whether they're toddlers or teens, kids crave emotional security. You don't need to be their best friend, but you do need to be their safe place.

Coaching Tip: Define what success looks like in your parenting.

- Is it raising respectful kids?
- Growing their faith?
- Building emotional honesty?

Define it, then build with that vision in mind.

Fathers, do not provoke your children to anger {do not exasperate them to the point of resentment with demands that are trivial or unreasonable or humiliating or abusive; nor by showing favoritism or indifference to any of them}, but bring them up {tenderly, with lovingkindness} in the discipline and instruction of the Lord.
— *Ephesians 6:4, AMP*

2. Model the Life You Want Them to Live

Kids watch more than they listen. They might forget our lectures, but they'll remember how we treated the waitress, how we responded under pressure, how we forgave (or didn't). Are you living out the kindness, faith, integrity, and resilience you want to see in them?

Real-Life Practice: Choose a weekly family "value word" (like patience, gratitude, or courage). Talk about it at dinner, celebrate it when you see it, and practice it together.

"Our children may forget what we say, but they will always remember what we do."
— *Maya Angelou*

3. Presence Over Perfection

You don't have to have all the answers. What your children need most is your presence: your eyes, your ears, your time, your heart. It's the little moments that build trust.

Try This: Create "micro-moments" of connection: a silly dance party before bed, a distraction-free car ride, or a shared snack on the porch. These simple minutes often become the big memories.

You shall teach them {diligently} to your children {impressing God's precepts on their minds and penetrating their hearts with His truths}, speaking of them when you sit in your house and when you walk along the road and when you lie down and when you rise up. — Deuteronomy 11:19, AMP

4. Speak Life, Daily and Intentionally

Your words will become your child's internal voice. Are you speaking more life than correction? Are you affirming their identity beyond their behavior?

Coaching Technique: The "3 Statements Rule": Say three uplifting things to each child every day. It doesn't have to be deep, just sincere. "I'm proud of you." "You make me smile." "God made you for amazing things."

5. Stay Calm in the Chaos

Parenting will stretch your patience like nothing else. But your peace carries power. Staying grounded in grace when everything feels unglued isn't just a reaction; it's a skill. And like any skill, it can be built, strengthened, and passed on.

Grace under pressure is the ability to remain calm, composed, and kind, even when you're under stress, facing chaos, or feeling emotionally overwhelmed. It's not about pretending everything is fine; it's about choosing your response rather than reacting out of frustration or fear.

Like any skill, it can be developed through self-awareness, emotional regulation, and intentional practices like deep breathing, prayer, or pausing before speaking. For moms especially, it becomes a powerful tool, teaching your children by example how to face life's hard moments with strength, softness, and spiritual grounding.

Coach's Reset Method:

- ☐ Pause: Take three deep breaths.
- ☐ Pray: "Lord, give me wisdom right now."
- ☐ Respond: With calm, not chaos.
- ☐ Reset: You can restart at any moment.

A gentle answer turns away wrath, but a harsh word stirs up anger.
— Proverbs 15:1, NIV

6. Create Moments That Matter

The best family memories usually aren't on the calendar; they're in the quiet, consistent showing up. What traditions can you start (or restart)? What joyful, silly, sacred memories are you making?

Try This: Create a "Family Fun Jar." Let each family member add activities, such as game night, an ice cream run, or a pajama breakfast. Pull one idea weekly and make it happen.

7. Parent From Overflow, Not Exhaustion

You can't pour into your children when your own tank is empty. You matter, sis. Your health, your heart, your healing, it all matters. When you care for yourself, you model wholeness for your kids.

Self-Care Check-In:

- ☐ Did I drink water and eat today?
- ☐ Did I pause to be with God?
- ☐ Did I rest, even briefly?
- ☐ Did I give myself grace?

Your well-being is not a luxury, it's a legacy.

8. Listen With Your Heart

Regardless of their age, children yearn to be heard. Are you creating space for their voice? Their feelings? Their dreams?

Try This: Replace closed questions with open ones. Ask, "What made you laugh today?" or "What's something you wish I understood?" These questions open the door to connection.

9. Parent With Vision, Not Just Reaction

The most powerful parents aren't just putting out fires. They're building futures. What kind of parent do you want to be remembered as? What kind of adults do you want to raise?

The righteous man who walks in integrity and lives life in accord with his {godly} beliefs—How blessed {happy and spiritually secure} are his children after him {who have his example to follow}. — Proverbs 20:7, AMP

Try This: Write out your parenting vision. Hang it somewhere visible. Speak it over your family. Legacy isn't built in one big moment but in a thousand little ones.

10. Today's Commitment: Lead With Love

End your day with reflection, not regret. Ask, "How did I love my child today? What can I do better tomorrow?" And then, *offer yourself grace.* Because where you fall short, God fills in the gaps.

Applying the GRACE Method:

☐ **G: Ground Yourself in God's Truth:** You are not raising your children alone. God is parenting you while you parent them. *(Study: Matthew 6:9-13, John 1:12, Romans 8:15, Galatians 4:6, Psalm 103:13).*

☐ **R: Reflect on Your Current Reality:** What season is your family in? What's working? What needs more intentional love?

☐ **A: Act With Intentional Steps:** Choose one practical idea from this chapter and apply it today, just one.

☐ **C: Create Consistent Systems:** Build routines and rhythms that support connection: bedtime blessings, family check-ins, mealtime prayers.

☐ **E: Embrace Progress Over Perfection:** Every day is a new opportunity. Show up with love, adjust as needed, and keep going.

Reflection Questions:

1. Which of these 10 principles do I need to focus on the most right now?
2. How would my children describe the way I love and lead them?
3. What small moment can I intentionally create this week?

4. In what ways can I care for myself better so that I can parent from a place of overflow?

A Powerful Prayer for the Parent:

Heavenly Father,

Thank You for trusting me with this sacred assignment of parenting. I confess that I don't always get it right. Some days I feel depleted, discouraged, or unsure. But I know You are the perfect Parent, and You promise to walk with me in every moment. Help me to see each child through Your eyes. Give me wisdom in my discipline, tenderness in my tone, and vision for the future I'm helping to build. Let my home be a place where love is spoken freely, mistakes are covered with grace, and faith is lived out in the ordinary.

In Jesus' name, Amen.

Encouragement for the Journey

You're doing better than you think. You're not raising robots; you're raising real, messy, magnificent human beings. And they are blessed to have you. Parenting isn't about getting every moment right; it's about showing up, again and again, with love. Keep going. Keep planting seeds. And know that the legacy you're building is already taking root.

BIBLICAL & EMPOWERMENT COACHING WORKSHEET FOR LOVING PARENTING

Practical Steps to Grow as a Present, Loving, and Spirit-Led Parent

1. Reflect on Your Parenting Vision

Train up a child in the way he should go {teaching him to seek God's wisdom and will for his abilities and talents}, even when he is old he will not depart from it.
— Proverbs 22:6, AMP

Prompt:

- What kind of parent do I want to be remembered as?

- What values do I want to pass down to my children?

Write your parenting mission statement below:

2. Evaluate the Emotional Climate of Your Home

Let everything you do be done in love {motivated and inspired by God's love for us}.
— 1 Corinthians 16:14, AMP

Checklist: Which of these are present in your parenting this week?

☐ I am quick to listen and slow to anger.
☐ I affirm more than I correct.
☐ I create time for laughter, hugs, and one-on-one time.
☐ I model emotional control and ask for forgiveness when I fall short of it.

Coaching Tip: Children thrive when they feel emotionally safe. Make your home a refuge, not a battlefield.

3. Connection Inventory: How Healthy Is Your Bond?

Fathers, do not provoke your children to anger {do not exasperate them to the point of resentment with demands that are trivial or unreasonable or humiliating or abusive; nor by showing favoritism or indifference to any of them}, but bring them up {tenderly, with lovingkindness} in the discipline and instruction of the Lord.
— Ephesians 6:4, AMP

For Each Child (or age group):

- Do they feel seen, heard, and loved by me?
- What's one thing I can do this week to deepen our connection?

Ideas for "Micro-Moments" of Connection:

☐ Share a bedtime blessing
☐ Go on a short walk and ask questions

☐ Give them a handwritten note
☐ Let them pick a dinner or family activity

4. Speak Life Daily

Death and life are in the power of the tongue, and those who love it and indulge it will eat its fruit and bear the consequences of their words.– Proverbs 18:21, AMP

3 Statements of Life Practice:

Say at least *three life-giving phrases* to your child each day.

Examples:

- "You make me proud."
- "God made you for something special."
- "I love the way you think."

Write three phrases you will say to each of your children today:

5. Set Values-Based Boundaries

How blessed and favored by God are those whose way is blameless {those with personal integrity, the upright, the guileless}, who walk in the law {and who are guided by the precepts and revealed will} of the Lord. – Psalm 119:1, AMP

Instead of long lists of rules, identify 3–5 *core family values* to guide discipline and daily expectations.

Examples:

- We tell the truth.
- We use our words kindly.
- We take care of our responsibilities.

List your family's top 3–5 values here:

6. Practice Calm Discipline

A soft and gentle and thoughtful answer turns away wrath, but harsh and painful and careless words stir up anger. – Proverbs 15:1, AMP

The Coach's Reset Method:

- ☐ Pause: Take three deep breaths
- ☐ Pray: Ask God for peace.
- ☐ Respond: With calm, not chaos.
- ☐ Reset: Try again if needed.

Coaching Tool: Don't escalate. Regulate. Be still. Your calm is contagious.

7. Care for the Parent (That's You!)

…'You shall {unselfishly} love your neighbor as yourself.' There is no other commandment greater than these."– Mark 12:31, AMP

Self-Care Mini Check-In:

- ☐ Did I hydrate and eat nourishing food today?
- ☐ Did I spend at least 5 minutes in God's presence?
- ☐ Did I rest, even briefly?
- ☐ Did I offer myself grace?

Reminder: You cannot pour love from an empty cup.

8. Empower, Don't Control

The righteous man who walks in integrity and lives life in accord with his {godly} beliefs—How blessed {happy and spiritually secure} are his children after him {who have his example to follow}. – Proverbs 20:7, AMP

Instead of: "Because I said so."

Try:

- "Let's figure this out together."
- "Here's why this matters."
- "What do you think a better choice might be?"

Write a script for one hard conversation you often have, using calm and respectful words:

9. Create a Legacy of Faith and Love

These words, which I am commanding you today, shall be {written} on your heart and mind. You shall teach them diligently to your children {impressing God's precepts on their minds and penetrating their hearts with His truths} and shall speak of them when you sit in your house and when you walk on the road and when you lie down and when you get up. — Deuteronomy 6:6–7, AMP

Ideas to nurture faith in your kids:

- Pray together each morning or night
- Talk about how you see God in everyday life.
- Share Bible stories that relate to real-life problems.
- Celebrate answered prayers together.

What's one faith practice you will add (or restore) this week?

Final Encouragement

You don't have to be a perfect parent, just a present one. Every prayer, hug, boundary, and bedtime blessing matters. You are doing holy work by loving your child well.

Affirmation: *"I am a loving, Spirit-led parent, growing in grace every day. God is guiding me, and His love flows through me into my family."*

CHAPTER 13

Relationships: Boundaries and Belonging

Bad company corrupts good character. — *1 Corinthians 15:33, NIV*

Let's begin with a truth that may feel both freeing and hard: Not everyone is meant to walk with you forever. And that's okay. Relationships are seasonal. As you grow, your relationships will shift. Some will deepen. Some will fade. And some may have to be lovingly released.

This isn't rejection. It's refinement.

It's God pruning your life with care so you can bear more fruit, walk in more peace, and be surrounded by people who honor the woman you're becoming.

Whether you're nurturing lifelong friendships, grieving a broken bond, or making space for healthier connections, this chapter is about reflecting on your relationships through the lens of purpose, peace, and spiritual alignment.

When Love Doesn't Feel Mutual

I once had a best friend for over fifteen years. I gave her my loyalty, my time, my secrets, and my support. But over time, I began to realize something painful: our relationship left me feeling smaller. Dismissed. Drained. When I shared joyful news, a new dream, a big win, she would pivot the conversation back to her own drama or respond with cynicism. For years, I told myself that being a "good friend" meant staying, serving, and sacrificing. But God showed me something greater: that love without boundaries isn't love at all.

The day I said, "I need space," she told me I was selfish and unforgiving. That conversation was excruciating. But it created space in my heart for healing and space in my life for life-giving friendships. Friendships that breathe faith into my calling and joy into my days, the same way I give and sow faith, joy, and love into others.

Sometimes letting go is an act of obedience. And sometimes, the most loving thing you can do is walk away.

Your Relationships Shape Your Legacy

Your relationships will either propel you into God's purpose or pull you from it. That's why it's important to regularly evaluate who has access to your heart, your energy, and your inner circle. Here's a framework to help you do just that.

The CIRCLE Method

A framework for evaluating, healing, and nurturing relationships.

C: Clarify Your Relationship Values: Before you build or rebuild any relationship, ask: What truly matters to me in a friendship or connection? Identify your non-negotiables.

Top 10 Qualities to Reflect On:

- ☐ Mutual respect
- ☐ Emotional safety
- ☐ Shared faith or values
- ☐ Honesty
- ☐ Reciprocity
- ☐ Encouragement
- ☐ Healthy conflict resolution
- ☐ Reliability
- ☐ Joy
- ☐ Space for individuality

Choose your top 5 non-negotiables. These will become your filter for future connections and your guide for healing current ones.

I: Identify Your Relationship Patterns: We all have tendencies that shape our relational habits. Some are healthy. Some need healing.

☐ The Over-Giver: Always gives, rarely receives.
☐ The People-Pleaser: Avoids conflict, hides true opinions.
☐ The Fixer: Feels responsible for everyone's healing.
☐ The Wall-Builder: Stays guarded, afraid of vulnerability.

Which one do you lean toward? Ask God to gently show you where you can grow.

R: Refine Your Inner Circle

Not every relationship is meant for the front row of your life.

The Relationship Circle System:

1. *Inner Circle:* Full access. Safe. Mutual.
2. *Support Circle:* Encouraging, but with limited access.
3. *Social Circle:* Friendly acquaintances. Surface-level.
4. *Distant Circle:* Necessary distance. Love from afar.

Audit your current relationships. Which ones need more nurturing? Which ones need new boundaries?

C: Communicate with Courage and Clarity

Speak the truth in love. Use grace and wisdom. Here's a method to guide hard conversations:

The PEACE Method:

☐ *Pause* to pray first.
☐ *Empathize* with their perspective.
☐ *Assert* your needs clearly.
☐ *Clarify* misunderstandings.
☐ *Engage* in solutions together.

Example Boundary Script:
"I care about you, and I want to be honest. When [behavior], I feel [emotion] because [impact]. Going forward, I need [boundary]. Can we talk about this together?"

L: Learn the Language of Healthy Boundaries
Boundaries aren't punishment. They're protection.

Examples:

1. *Physical:* Who can touch you or enter your space.
2. *Emotional:* What you will and won't tolerate.
3. *Time:* Availability for calls, texts, or visits.
4. *Spiritual:* What influences you allow near your faith.

Remember, "no" is a full sentence. And boundaries stated with love still honor God.

E: Evolve and Let Relationships Change

Some relationships are meant to be for a reason, a season, or a lifetime. Honor each one for what it is. When it's time to move on, do so with grace.

Signs It's Time to Let Go:

- Consistent exhaustion or anxiety after interacting
- Repeated boundary violations
- Diminished self-worth or joy

Prayer for Release:

Lord,
    If this relationship no longer honors You or serves my purpose, give me the strength to release it with grace. Heal what's broken and protect what's purposeful and sacred. I trust Your character, Your intentions, and that You have good plans for my life. Let Your Kingdom come and let Your will be done on earth as it is in Heaven, in my life and relationships.
    In Jesus' Name, Amen.

The Heart of Loving Well

Relationships reflect the character of God; His desire for connection, His call to love, and His grace for imperfection. But they also require intention. Here are some necessary intentional actions for your relationships:

- Speak life even when it's hard.
- Show up even when it's inconvenient.
- Forgive even when it's not asked.
- Set boundaries even when it's uncomfortable.

You don't have to be everything to everyone. You just need to be faithful to what God called you to be: a woman who loves with grace and stands with truth.

Friend, the way you love, the people you choose, and the boundaries you uphold will shape not only your peace but your legacy. So love boldly, communicate honestly, and walk in the confidence that God is guiding every connection.

Applying the GRACE Method to Your Relationships

☐ **G: Ground Yourself in God's Truth:** You were created for relationships, not with everyone, but with the right ones. God calls us to love deeply, set boundaries wisely, and reflect His heart in every interaction.

As iron sharpens iron, so one person sharpens another. — Proverbs 27:17, NIV

☐ **R: Reflect on Your Current Reality:** Which relationships energize you? Which ones deplete you? What patterns keep showing up? Take an honest look at who has access to your time, energy, and heart.

☐ **A: Act with Intentional Steps:** Choose one relationship to nurture or redefine this week. Maybe it's a heartfelt conversation, a boundary you need to express, or simply sending encouragement. Take the step.

☐ **C: Create Consistent Systems:** Build rhythms that support healthy relationships, including weekly check-ins with your spouse, monthly friend dates, and scheduled alone time for reflection and prayer. Consistency deepens connection.

☐ **E: Embrace Progress Over Perfection:** You're not called to be the perfect friend, sister, wife, or mentor, just a present and prayerful one. Every healthy relationship is a work in progress, and every step you take matters.

Reflection Questions

1. What relationships in my life feel life-giving, and which ones feel draining?
2. Where might God be inviting me to set a new boundary or have an honest conversation?
3. What patterns do I notice in how I show up in relationships, and where can I make improvements?
4. Who can I reach out to this week with intentional encouragement or support?
5. How do I want to be remembered in the hearts of those I love?

A Powerful Prayer for Your Relationships

Heavenly Father,

Thank You for the people You've placed in my life, for the ones who love me, challenge me, and walk with me. Help me to reflect Your heart in every interaction. Teach me to be both loving and wise, gentle and bold. Show me where to release what no longer serves Your purpose and where to fight for what truly matters.

Strengthen my ability to set healthy boundaries without guilt and to offer grace without enabling harm. God, I place every relationship (past, present, and future) into Your hands. Heal what's broken. Protect what's sacred. Open doors for new, life-giving connections that align with Your will.

And most of all, shape me to be a friend, sister, wife, or mentor who radiates Your love.

In Jesus' name, Amen.

CHAPTER 14

Career/Business: Purpose and Profit Can Coexist

Commit to the Lord whatever you do, and He will establish your plans.
— *Proverbs 16:3, NIV*

I recall a night when everything felt overwhelming. I was trying to fold laundry *again* (a never-ending task with a family of nine), send an email, finish dinner as we had returned home late from a sports event, and plan content for a new book, all at the same time. The house was loud, my heart was tired, and tears were falling before I even realized I was crying. My husband walked in, looked at me, and said, "You don't have to do it all tonight."

But that was the thing, I wasn't just trying to do it all. I was trying to be it all: a faithful wife, a present mom, a successful entrepreneur, a prayerful daughter and sister, a good friend, a coach, a chef, a housekeeper, and a vision carrier. And I know I'm not alone. Many women, especially moms, are navigating their careers, callings, and dreams while feeling like something important or even critical has to be sacrificed.

What if you didn't have to choose? Not between purpose and peace. Not between your paycheck and your calling. Not between being a present, powerful mother and building something meaningful beyond your home.

You were never meant to hustle yourself into exhaustion just to leave a legacy. Your business, your career, your creativity, all of it can become an act of worship when offered back to God. You were made to build, not just homes but hope. Not just routines but revival. Not just income but impact.

If you're constantly feeling burned out, chances are you've been operating apart from divine strategy, moving in survival mode instead of alignment and wisdom. But here's the good news: when you reconnect with your Creator and invite Him to be your CEO, everything changes. Peace returns. Clarity follows. And you begin to build with purpose, on purpose, while still enjoying your everyday life.

You were made for more, and you can walk in both purpose and profit, without losing your soul. Let's take that journey together.

1. Career Heart Check: Are You Thriving or Just Surviving?

Where there is no vision, the people perish… — Proverbs 29:18, KJV

What is your vision for your career or business? Ask yourself: Does this work bring me joy? Fulfillment? Alignment? On a scale from 1 to 10, rate yourself in these five areas:

____Purpose
____Impact
____Income
____Flexibility
____Joy

What's one change you could make this month to raise one of those scores by just one point?

2. Aligning Passion with Purpose

Your passions were not randomly assigned. They are clues to your calling. Reflect on what excites you, what angers you, and what problems you feel called to solve. When your gifts meet a need, you've found purpose.

Each of you should use whatever gift you have received to serve others, as faithful stewards of God's grace in its various forms. — 1 Peter 4:10, NIV

Empowerment Equation:
Passion + Purpose + People + Profit = Calling Worth Pursuing

Take 10 minutes this week to journal about each part of the *Empowerment Equation*, what lights you up, and who you feel called to serve. Then, begin planning how you will progress forward into your future endeavors.

3. Celebrate Your God-Given Strengths

Let's stop downplaying what comes naturally to you.

Ask:
- What do people consistently thank me for or come to me for help with?
- What have I always done well, even without formal training?
- What do you do with ease that others struggle with?

These aren't accidents. They are assignments.

Whether it's speaking, organizing, problem-solving, creating, or nurturing, those aren't just "nice things" about you. Those are tools God has placed in you to bless the world. You are not bragging when you name your gifts; you are stewarding them.

Coaching Tip: Make a *"Strength Inventory."* List five strengths, and next to each one, write how it could be used to help someone else or solve a problem.

4. Redefining What Success Really Means

The world says success is about hustle, comparison, and going bigger. God says success is about being obedient and aligned with Him.

Ask:
- What does success look like for me in this season?
- Does my current work align with my values and vision for life?

Success, in God's eyes, isn't about how high you climb. It's about how well you walk with Him on the journey. Real success is when your goals align with God's guidance.

Reflection Prompt: "Lord, help me release the pressure to impress and embrace the peace of walking in purpose."

Better a little with righteousness than much gain with injustice.
— Proverbs 16:8, NIV

5. Small Beginnings, Big Futures

Whether you're clocking in at work or sketching out your dreams by moonlight after everyone's asleep, this season matters. Don't dismiss it. Don't rush past it. Steward it with intention.

Because how you show up in the small things today is laying the foundation for something greater tomorrow.

You may not be in your dream role yet. You might be balancing diapers and deadlines, caregiving and career goals, wondering if your vision will ever come to fruition. But hear this: your current season isn't wasted, it's a training ground. Every act of faithfulness, every sacrifice, every step you take right now is preparing you for what's next.

Do not despise these small beginnings, for the Lord rejoices to see the work begin.
— Zechariah 4:10, NLT

God celebrates your start. So keep going. Even the midnight movement toward your goals has purpose when it's in His hands.

6. Stewarding Your Time and Energy Wisely

You cannot do it all, and that's okay. You were never meant to. So, instead of doing more, try doing what matters most.

Ask: What do I need to finish, delegate, or release to create more peace and productivity? Ask God for guidance and strategy about all of it.

Coach's Time Management Tool: The 3D System

1. **Do it** now if it's aligned and urgent.
2. **Delegate** it if someone else can do it.
3. **Drop it** if it no longer fits your season.

Manage your time with grace, not guilt. Create a "Stop -Doing List" to go with your "To-Do List".

7. Grow Intentionally: Committing to Personal Growth

If you want to increase your income, expand your impact, or step into something new, you have to be willing to grow.

Ask yourself:
- What's one skill I need to sharpen this season?
- What do I need to study, read, or practice to go to my next level?

Take the class, listen to the podcast, read the book, and keep learning. Equipped women become empowered women.

The wise will hear and increase their learning, and the person of understanding will acquire wise counsel and the skill {to steer his course wisely and lead others to the truth}, —Proverbs 1:5, AMP

8. Surround Yourself With Builders

You need people who speak life into your dreams, who challenge you, who make you think bigger. Pray for mentors, cheerleaders, and truth-tellers. You are not meant to build alone. Join a community, mastermind, or business Bible study group. Isolation is the enemy of inspiration.

God uses people to open doors, challenge your thinking, and sharpen your skills. So, surround yourself with the right people. Don't isolate; build your support circle.

Your "Growth Circle" Should Include:

☐ **A mentor** who's been where you want to go
☐ **A peer** who challenges and encourages you
☐ **A group or community** that aligns with your goals

Pray for divine connections. God knows who belongs on your journey.

Plans fail for lack of counsel, but with many advisers they succeed.
— Proverbs 15:22, NIV

9. Creating Impact That Outlives You

Your work isn't just about the present; it's about the legacy you're leaving.

Ask:

- How can I create lasting value?
- What story do I want my business, career, or work ethic to tell when I'm gone?

Let your light shine before others, that they may see your good deeds and glorify your Father in heaven. — Matthew 5:16, NIV

You were made to multiply, not just income but impact. What you're building now can become a blessing for generations to come. So, build to bless, not just impress. Let your work reflect the goodness of God. Think generationally. What impact will your effort today have on your family, your community, or your legacy?

10. Start Small, Start Now

Purpose isn't a place you arrive at. It's a path you walk daily. Start with one step. One action. One "yes."

Ask:

- What one action can I take today that honors my calling?
- How can I show up today as the woman I'm becoming?

Today's Affirmation: *"I walk in purpose. I build with passion. I trust God's plan. I am worthy of the success He has for me."*

Final Encouragement:

Dear sister, your career or business isn't just about a title or a check. It's about walking in your God-given calling with courage, grace, and obedience. Whether you're leading teams or leading toddlers, teaching classes or launching a course, you're doing divine, purposeful work. Don't downplay your gifts. Don't shrink back.

You're not behind, you're being prepared. So, keep going. Keep building. Keep believing. You can thrive. You can prosper. And you can do it all with peace of mind. Purpose and profit really can coexist when God is your CEO.

Applying the GRACE Method

☐ **G: Ground Yourself in God's Truth:** Remember that your calling is sacred.

☐ **R: Reflect on Your Current Reality:** Where are you thriving? Where are you striving?

☐ **A: Act With Intentional Steps:** Make one small move toward your God-given dream this week.

☐ **C: Create Consistent Systems:** Utilize simple tools to manage your time, money, and energy effectively.

☐ **E: Embrace Progress Over Perfection:** You don't need to have it all figured out to move forward.

Reflection Questions

1. What dream or vision has God placed on your heart?
2. In what ways have you been playing small out of fear?
3. What strengths can you celebrate and use to bless others this week?
4. What does success look like to you in this season?
5. Who are the people you need to surround yourself with for your next level?

Powerful Prayer for the Builder

Heavenly Father,

Thank You for giving me gifts, dreams, and divine assignments. When I feel torn between motherhood or womanhood and mission, remind me that You created me for both. Help me to walk in purpose, not pressure. Lead me with wisdom. Equip me with strategy. Surround me with support. And give me courage to pursue the vision You placed in my heart, not just for my own success, but to bless others and bring glory to You. I trust You as my CEO, my Provider, and my Strength.

In Jesus' name, Amen.

You don't have to choose between thriving and trusting God. You can do both. Purpose and profit can coexist when faith leads the way.

CHAPTER 15

Education: Stay Curious, Stay Growing

Let the wise listen and add to their learning, and let the discerning get guidance.
— Proverbs 1:5, NIV

Sweet sister, let me speak to the woman inside you who may have forgotten just how capable, curious, and called she really is. That nudge you've been feeling, the desire to learn, to grow, to expand, isn't just a passing thought. It's a divine invitation. No matter what season you're in, whether you're raising toddlers, managing teenagers, transitioning careers, or rediscovering yourself after years of pouring into others, your education journey is not behind you. It's alive and waiting.

You Are Not Too Late. You Are Right On Time.

We often think of education as something tied to a classroom or achieving obtaining a degree. And you are fully capable of accomplishing that, but true learning is so much more. It's the posture of a teachable heart, the decision to stay curious, and the courage to say, "I'm not done growing." It's discovering that God is always revealing more, not just about the world, but about who you are and who you're becoming.

Whether you're brushing up on professional skills, diving deeper into God's Word, learning alongside your children, or exploring a new hobby just for joy, every step forward matters. You don't need a traditional school to enroll in the curriculum of becoming who and what you desire to be. And you don't need permission to pursue the growth God has placed on your heart.

Start With Self-Reflection

CREATE THE LIFE YOU WANT NOW

Ask yourself:

- Where in my life do I feel stagnant?
- What new skills or insights could breathe life into my work, my family, or my walk with God?
- What have I always wanted to learn, but felt too afraid, too old, or too overwhelmed to pursue?

Maybe it's learning how to manage your finances better, how to study Scripture more deeply, or how to finally start that blog, business, or book. That curiosity is sacred. Don't ignore it.

Wise people treasure knowledge. — Proverbs 10:14, NLT

Empowerment Coaching Tip

Try a Growth Audit:

1. What do I already know and do well?
2. What would I love to learn next?
3. What's one small, simple step I can take this week to get started?

Follow Your Curiosity

Learning should never feel like punishment; it should feel like play. Ask yourself: What lights me up? What makes me lose track of time? God often hides purpose inside our passions. If you love writing, baking, design, or even organizing, you may be holding a seed of something bigger.

Try This: Make a *"Learning Joy List."* Write down 10 topics you'd love to explore. Circle the one that excites you most and commit to reading, watching, or practicing something related to it this month.

Make Learning a Lifestyle

Sis, you don't need hours a day. You need intention.

- ☐ Listen to a podcast while driving or doing dishes.
- ☐ Watch a 10-minute video during your lunch break.

☐ Read 10 pages of a book each night before bed.
☐ Study one Scripture a day with a journal and pen.
☐ Learn something new with your kids or spouse and let growth become a family value.

The heart of the discerning acquires knowledge, for the ears of the wise seek it out.
— *Proverbs 18:15, NIV*

Empowered Learning Tip: Set a goal to take one online course, read one full book, or master one new skill every 90 days. Document your learning and celebrate your progress.

Conquer the Learning Curve with Grace

New things can be intimidating. But the fear of looking foolish should never outweigh the joy of becoming better. You don't have to know it all, you just have to begin.

Coach Strategy: The 15-Minute Rule

Commit to just 15 minutes a day of intentional learning: reading, listening, practicing, or watching. Over time, these small daily deposits yield extraordinary growth.

Do not despise these small beginnings, for the Lord rejoices to see the work begin.
— *Zechariah 4:10, NLT*

Learn on Purpose, with Purpose

The goal of growth is not just knowledge, it's transformation. Ask yourself:

• How will this help me serve my family better?
• How can this be used to glorify God or help someone else?
• What doors might this open if I stay faithful to it?

When I first stepped into coaching, I had no blueprint. I just knew I needed something more. I took one class, read one book, and committed one hour a week to learning, and over time, it turned into a life of purpose

CREATE THE LIFE YOU WANT NOW

and impact. What could it do for you?

Take Ownership of Your Growth

Your next level won't happen by accident. Make space for it. Guard it like your health. Ask your family to support you in this. Why? Because your growth blesses them, too.

Coaching Tip: Block out "Growth Time" in your calendar weekly. Whether it's 30 minutes on Sunday night or a few minutes daily, protect that space. Put it on the calendar like an appointment with your destiny.

Faith without works is dead. — *James 2:20, AMP*

Stay Rooted in Your "Why"

Motivation fades. The podcasts, the courses, the shiny new journals… they all lose their sparkle when life gets loud. When the meals need prepared, the kids are calling, work is demanding, a loved one requires your hands-on care, and your energy feels depleted, it's not your to-do list that will carry you through. It's your *why*.

Your "why" is the soul of your growth journey. It's what anchors you when the waves of distraction, discouragement, and doubt start rising. It's the truth that fuels you when no one else sees the effort you're putting in. It's the internal fire that whispers, "Keep going. It matters."

So pause, and ask yourself with honesty and compassion:

1. **Who am I becoming through this process?** Not just what am I doing, but who am I becoming in character, in confidence, in calling?
2. **Why does this matter to me deeply?** Go beyond the surface. Is it about freedom? Healing? Restoring a part of yourself that felt forgotten? Equipping yourself to bless others?
3. **How does this help me fulfill my calling?** Your calling may not be flashy or public, but it is God-given and holy. Whether it's leading a team, loving your children well, writing words that heal, or simply becoming more whole, this matters to God.
4. **What legacy will this build for my family and the women com-

ing behind me?

Sis, your growth plants seeds. Your commitment to learn creates ripple effects in your children, your community, and even women you'll never meet. You are building a legacy of wisdom, strength, and intentionality, and legacy isn't left for later; it's built now.

You don't have to have all the answers, but you do need to remember the reason. Because your "why" will do what sheer willpower can't. It will get you out of bed. It will remind you that this hard moment can still work together and be used for your good and God's glory. It will help you say no to distractions and yes to destiny. It will push you to grow not just for yourself, but for the lives attached to your obedience.

> *She sets about her work vigorously; her arms are strong for her tasks.*
> — *Proverbs 31:17, NIV*

This woman, this Proverbs 31 woman, is not superhuman. She's rooted. She's driven by something bigger than the task at hand. Her strength is not just physical; it's spiritual. And so is yours.

So write down your why. Keep it visible. Tape it to your mirror. Put it in your planner. Pray over it daily. And let it become the divine reminder that fuels your forward motion, especially when the excitement wears off.

Because a woman with a clear "why" cannot be stopped. She's not just learning, she's becoming who God created and called her to be. And that, sweet friend, is unstoppable power in motion.

Partner With God in the Process

God is the ultimate teacher. He will guide your mind and your steps. Ask Him for divine strategy and to lead you to the right resources, mentors, and moments of clarity.

Prayer:

Lord,

Thank You for the capacity You've given me to learn and grow. Help me steward this gift well. Lead me to the right knowledge at the right time.

Give me the confidence to overcome my doubts and the grace to persevere through the hard times. May my growth bring honor to You and bless everyone around me.

In Jesus' name, Amen.

If any of you lacks wisdom, let him ask of God... and it will be given to him.
—*James 1:5, NKJV*

Final Encouragement

Beautiful sister, your mind is a miracle. God designed you with the ability to grow, stretch, and adapt at any age, in any season. Never stop learning. Never stop seeking wisdom. Never stop believing in what's possible for you. Because when you grow, your confidence grows. Your opportunities multiply. And your impact expands. Stay curious. Stay growing. And stay rooted in the truth that learning is not just a task; it's an act of faith.

Applying the GRACE Method to Your Growth

Let this be your rhythm for learning, not perfection:

☐ **G: Ground Yourself in God's Truth:** Learning isn't just about personal development; it's about spiritual stewardship. Ask God to guide your mind as you grow. His wisdom is your foundation.

☐ **R: Reflect on Your Current Reality:** Where do you feel stagnant? Where is your curiosity nudging you? Be honest without shame. Growth begins with truth.

☐ **A: Act with Intentional Steps:** Start small. Choose one topic, one podcast, or one class. Focus on progress, not perfection.

☐ **C: Create Consistent Systems:** Create a daily or weekly "growth space." Tie it to a routine (such as coffee, lunch, or bedtime) and make it easy to show up.

☐ **E: Embrace Progress Over Perfection:** You don't need to know it all today. Celebrate your commitment. Learning is a journey, and every step counts.

Reflection Questions

1. What area of growth has God been gently nudging you toward?
2. What limiting belief has held you back from learning something new?
3. What small action can you take this week to begin your growth journey?
4. Who in your life could benefit from what you're learning?
5. How does your learning align with the legacy you want to leave?

A Powerful Prayer for the Growing Woman

Heavenly Father,

Thank You for the incredible mind You've given me and the opportunity to grow. Help me silence the lies that say I'm too old, too late, or too busy. Fill me with confidence, curiosity, and a hunger for wisdom. Lead me to the right books, the right videos and course, the right mentors, and the right moments to learn. May I grow not just in knowledge, but in character, in purpose, and in faith. I surrender my growth journey to You. Shape me into the woman You created me to be for my family, my community, and Your kingdom.

In Jesus' mighty name, Amen.

CHAPTER 16

Physical Health: Honor the Body That Carries Your Calling

Health Disclaimer: This chapter is for inspirational purposes only and is not a substitute for medical advice. Please consult your doctor or healthcare team before making any changes to your health, fitness, or nutrition routines.

Your Body is Holy Ground

Do you not know that your body is a temple of the Holy Spirit, who is in you, whom you have received from God? You are not your own; you were bought at a price. Therefore, honor God with your bodies. —1 Corinthians 6:19–20, NIV

Let that sink in for a moment: your body is holy ground. Not something to criticize or neglect. Not a project to perfect. Not a number to shrink or shape. It is the sacred space God Himself chose to dwell in. That means your physical well-being is not a vanity metric; it is spiritual stewardship.

I will never forget the afternoon (after several weeks of recovering from having one of my children), when I couldn't catch my breath just walking up the stairs of the bleachers at one of my kids' games. My heart raced, my chest burned, and I had to sit down once I reached the top, taking deep breaths to calm my heart rate. I realized something sobering: I had been pouring out for everyone else and completely ignoring my vessel. The body God gave me to serve, love, and live in was suffering from my lack of self-care.

As a wife and mom of many, I know how easy it is to sacrifice your own wellness for the sake of your family. I've skipped meals, skipped sleep, skipped showers, even, in the name of "just getting through the day." But slowly, God began to show me: caring for my body is not selfish. It's critically important. It's God's divine plan, and it's a form of gratitude for life. It's how I honor the temple where He resides.

Why Physical Health Matters to Your Purpose

This isn't just about chasing a number on the scale or squeezing into a certain dress size. It's about being able to fully show up for the life God has called you to live. It's about energy and having the strength to get through your day without feeling drained before lunch. It's about clarity and being mentally present and emotionally available for the people you love. And it's about joy and being able to move, laugh, dance, and breathe deeply without pain or fatigue holding you back.

Your body is the vessel that carries your calling. When you feel sluggish, sick, or disconnected from your physical self, it's much harder to engage your spiritual gifts, walk in purpose, or enjoy the blessings you've been praying for. Physical health doesn't replace spiritual depth, but it can support it. A healthy body creates margin, deposits for future patience, creativity, service, play, and productivity. It allows you to be both available and vibrant for your spouse, your kids, your business, your ministry, and your dreams.

Maybe no one told you this before, but you are allowed to feel good in your body. You are allowed to prioritize your energy without guilt. You are allowed to move, eat, and rest in ways that restore you, not just because it helps others, but because you matter too.

When you're exhausted, everything feels harder. You're more likely to snap in frustration, withdraw from connection, procrastinate on your goals, and doubt your worth. But when your body is fueled, hydrated, rested, and strengthened, your confidence rises. You think clearly. You speak kindly. You show up fuller. You lead stronger. That's not vanity; it's vitality. And it's God's plan for your life.

Empowerment Tip: When your body is aligned with your calling, you feel more grounded, focused, and confident. You're not constantly trying to pour from an empty cup. You become a vessel overflowing with life, ready to pour into your children, your work, your ministry, and yourself, without burning out.

A happy heart is good medicine and a joyful mind causes healing, but a broken spirit dries up the bones. — Proverbs 17:22, AMP

You were never meant to serve from a place of unhappiness and depletion. God delights in seeing you thrive in strength, in health, and in peace. He formed your body not just to survive, but to move with power, rest with trust, and live with intention. So let's care for it, not with shame or striving, but with reverence and joy.

Define Success and Practice Body Grace

Let's pause right here and settle this in your heart: **You are worthy now.** Not ten pounds from now. Not once your skin clears, your schedule opens up, or your leggings fit differently. Not when your grocery list is perfectly organic or your steps hit 10,000 a day. **Right now. As you are. In this moment.**

Your worth is not a reward for achieving physical perfection; it's a reflection of who created you. You are already fearfully and wonderfully made. God didn't wait for a future version of you to declare your value. He chose you, He sees you, and He delights in you right now.

So let's take the pressure off. This journey is not about shrinking your body; it's about expanding your joy, your strength, and your capacity to thrive in the life you've been given. It's not about punishing yourself into change. It's about partnering with God to steward the vessel He has entrusted to you with compassion.

Coaching Reflection:

What if you stopped trying to be "disciplined" and started trying to be devoted? Not to a weight loss goal, but to the woman you're becoming and to the God who created you, one small, grace-filled step at a time.

Start from love, not shame. Start by asking:

- What does success in my health journey look like in this season?
- What would it mean to feel strong, steady, and supported in my body?
- How can I show myself the same tenderness I give to others?
- How can I define progress in ways that aren't just scale-based, but soul-based?

Maybe success is having enough energy to play with your kids in the yard. Perhaps it's drinking more water this week than last. Maybe it's saying no to burnout, and yes to a walk at sunset. Perhaps it's choosing rest without guilt.

Affirmation for This Season:

- "I honor my body as the vessel God gave me."
- "I will be gentle with myself as I grow."
- "I am fearfully and wonderfully made, in every season, at every size, and through every stage."

Friend, *body grace* means recognizing that progress may be slow, and it may be non-linear, but it is still a beautiful journey. Body grace means celebrating effort, not just outcome. It means embracing your reflection without criticism and thanking God for your body carrying you through every day, every burden, every miracle.

You are not behind. You are building your physical health daily. And building takes time. So keep showing up, not out of pressure, but out of purpose. Your body doesn't need perfection; it needs partnership and consistency. And your Creator is walking with you every step of the way.

Worthy Now

Again, **you are worthy** (of all good things, people, and experiences) **now.** Not ten pounds from now. Not when your calendar clears up. Not when your jeans fit differently. Right now. Start from love, not shame. Ask yourself: What does success in my health journey look like in this season? How can I be tender with myself while growing stronger?

Joy-Filled Movement

Let's shift the way we think about movement. This isn't about punishment. This isn't about "earning" your food or chasing an image on a magazine cover. This is about celebrating the amazing body God gave you and inviting more joy, energy, and freedom into your life.

You don't need a gym membership, fancy equipment, or a Pinterest-worthy fitness plan. What you need is permission to move your body in ways that feel good, doable, and delightful in this season.

Think of movement as worship. As a way to say, "Thank You, God, for this body that breathes, bends, and serves my family and calling."

Movement can be dancing barefoot in your kitchen to your favorite worship song.

It can be as simple as walking and talking with God around your neighborhood. It can be stretching in your living room while your toddler stacks blocks beside you. It can be playing tag with your kids or cleaning with purpose and praise music blaring in the background.

The goal isn't to break a sweat every day; it's to break free from the mindset that movement must be hard, harsh, or exhausting to "count." Movement can be peaceful. Movement can be joyful. Movement can be healing, and movement can be heavenly.

Strengthen Yourself for the Journey

She sets about her work vigorously; her arms are strong for her tasks.
— *Proverbs 31:17, NIV*

This verse reminds us that strength and stamina are integral to our calling. Not so we can "look good" by the world's standards, but so we can live well by God's design.

If movement feels overwhelming or if your schedule is packed, start small. 10 minutes. That's all you need to start shifting your mindset and building a rhythm.

- A walk around the block while listening to scripture or affirmations.
- A stretching session before bed to calm your nervous system.
- A dance break between meetings or homeschool lessons.
- A few wall push-ups or squats while waiting for dinner to finish.

It's not about doing everything, just doing something.

Empowerment Reminder:

Small movements lead to big victories. They build confidence. They boost mood. They create momentum. And most of all, they remind you that your body was made to move, not made to sit in shame.

So don't worry about being perfect. Just get moving. With joy. With purpose. With gratitude. Because when movement becomes an expression of joy instead of a punishment, it becomes sustainable. And when it's sustainable, it becomes powerful.

You don't need to hit the gym or buy fancy equipment to feel better in your body. Movement can be worship. Movement can be love. Dance in the kitchen. Take a prayer walk. Play tag with your little ones. When movement is joyful, it becomes sustainable.

Coach Tip: Start with just 10 minutes. A walk. A stretch. A dance break. Small movements lead to big victories.

Build a Sustainable Rhythm

Let go of the lie that it has to be all or nothing to count. One of the biggest reasons many women give up on their wellness goals is that they think if they can't look like a model in five seconds, dedicate an hour at the gym everyday, prepare picture-perfect meals for the week, or follow a detailed plan to the letter, then they might as well not even try.

But that's not how transformation works. That's not how God works either. You don't need perfect. You need routines and rhythm. A rhythm of grace. A rhythm that meets you in the chaos and honors your capacity in this season. A rhythm that reminds you that your wellness isn't a race; it's a relationship. With your body. With your Creator. And with your purpose.

Start with grace, not guilt. Start with "something," not everything. That "something" could be this: *The 10-10-10 Plan.* A simple, sacred routine that gently nourishes your body, mind, and spirit, all in 30 minutes or less.

The 10-10-10 Plan

10 Minutes of Joyful Movement

This could be walking, dancing, stretching, or doing a quick workout video. It's not about intensity; it's about intentionality. Move your body in a way that feels energizing, life-giving, and sustainable. Movement is medicine, and joy is fuel.

10 Minutes of Prayerful Stillness or Stretching

Carve out this time to reconnect with your breath and with God. Lay on the floor and breathe deeply. Read a scripture. Journal. Pray. Meditate on a promise. Or simply be still and quiet. This moment of presence will anchor your spirit in peace and remind you that you're not doing this alone.

10 Minutes of Simple Meal Prep

Don't overcomplicate it. Chop some veggies. Set out ingredients for tomorrow's breakfast. Pack a nourishing snack. You're not planning a feast, you're just preparing for one good decision ahead of time. These micro-prep moments build momentum and make healthy choices easier in the long run.

This is not about control; it's about care. Again, it's not about punishing your body; it's about partnering with your body. You are the steward of the vessel that carries your anointing. That deserves intentional rhythm, not relentless hustle.

What Rhythm Might Look Like in Real Life:

- ☐ Morning: 10-minute walk before the kids wake up
- ☐ Midday: 10-minute breath prayer and back stretch after lunch
- ☐ Evening: 10 minutes prepping tomorrow's lunch and water bottle

Or:

- ☐ Nap time power block: All 30 minutes in a row while the house is quiet
- ☐ Evening reset: After bedtime, before you collapse on the couch

There's no one "right" way. There's just your way. And the rhythm that's right for you in this season.

Coach Tip: Build this rhythm like you would a new habit: link it to something you already do.

- • "After I pour my coffee, I walk for 10 minutes."
- • "After I put the kids to bed, I prep my meals."
- • "After I brush my teeth, I stretch and breathe."

You don't have to do everything today. But you can do something. And that something, done with consistency, grace, and joy, will change everything over time. Your body is a temple. These 30 minutes are your offering.

Nourish Without Guilt

Sweet friend, you don't have to punish yourself through food to be healthy. God never designed eating to be a battlefield. From the Garden of Eden to the wedding feast in Revelation, nourishment was always meant to be both physical and spiritual. A gift to enjoy, not a problem to control.

You don't need to follow a fad diet or eliminate everything that brings you joy. What you need is freedom. Freedom to fuel your body with wisdom. Freedom to enjoy meals without shame. Freedom to choose what honors your energy, your body, and your purpose in this season.

Ask yourself gently:

1. What foods make me feel alive, not sluggish?
2. What meals bring me joy and nourishment?
3. How can I partner with the Holy Spirit to make choices that align with the woman I'm becoming?

Instead of obsessing over what you "can't" eat, begin focusing on what you can add:

- Add more water to hydrate your mind and body
- Add more vegetables for vibrant energy
- Add lean proteins to build strength
- Add whole grains to sustain you through your busy day
- Add small moments of gratitude before each meal to express thankfulness and to remind yourself this is not about perfection, it's about presence

Fuel for Your Calling

Food is fuel for your calling. It's not just about fitting into jeans; it's about having the energy to play with your kids, to write that book, to serve in ministry, to walk in your purpose with clarity and confidence. When your body is well-nourished, your spirit feels stronger too. Let's reframe nutrition as an act of worship. Each bite can be an opportunity to say, "Thank You, God, for this gift of life and health."

So whether you eat or drink or whatever you do, do it all for the glory of God.
—1 Corinthians 10:31, NIV

Let every meal be a reminder: You're not feeding shame, you're feeding strength. You're not chasing a diet, you're walking in daily devotion. You don't have to earn your worth. You're already worthy. Now it's time to nourish that worth with intention, love, and grace.

Hydration: A Simple Way to Heal and Glow from Within

Water isn't just a health tip; it's a healing practice. Your body is composed of approximately 60% water, and every system within it relies on proper hydration to function properly. From your brain to your skin, your digestion to your mood, water is God's built-in wellness tool, simple, accessible, and powerful.

Think of water as liquid grace. It flushes out what's toxic, brings clarity where there's brain fog, restores energy, and even enhances your natural beauty. When you're well-hydrated, your skin glows, your mind is sharper, your cravings decrease, and your joints and muscles move with ease. It's one of the kindest things you can do for yourself each day.

Wellness truth: Many of the things we blame on exhaustion, aging, or even anxiety, like headaches, fatigue, brain fog, irritability, or dry skin, can often be traced back to simple dehydration.

Faith-Filled Hydration Mindset

Hydration is more than a task on your to-do list, it's an act of stewardship. You are a temple of the Holy Spirit, and water is part of how you cleanse and care for that temple physically and spiritually.

But whoever drinks the water I give them will never thirst. Indeed, the water I give
them will become in them a spring of water welling up to eternal life."
—John 4:14, NIV

Let that verse remind you: drinking water isn't just about quenching physical thirst, it's symbolic of receiving life-giving refreshment from the Source Himself.

Hydration Habits That Heal

1. Start Your Morning With Water
Drink a full glass of water before coffee or tea. It wakes up your organs, jumpstarts your metabolism, and rehydrates you after a good night's sleep.

2. Flavor It Naturally
Not a fan of plain water? Add sliced lemon, cucumber, mint, or berries to make it feel like a spa treat, because you're worth it.

3. Pair Water With Routine

Link water intake to existing habits:
- Before brushing your teeth, drink a glass of water.
- Before each meal, sip water.
- Feeling stressed? Take 10 sips before you speak or react.

4. Use a Water Bottle You Love
Buy one that fits your personality. Cute. Classy. Inspiring. Let it serve as a visual cue and constant reminder: this is part of your healing process.

5. Set a Gentle Reminder
Use phone alarms or apps to nudge you throughout the day. Not to guilt you, but to lovingly remind you that you are worthy of care.

Beautiful From the Inside Out

Did you know that staying hydrated supports:

- Clearer skin and fewer breakouts
- Shinier hair and stronger nails
- Improved digestion and metabolism
- Reduced cravings and emotional eating

- Balanced mood and better sleep
- Less bloating and more energy

This is your permission to care for your beauty and well-being with no shame. Hydration is one of the easiest and most impactful ways to feel better, move better, and glow brighter.

Hydration Boost Challenge:

Try these 3 steps each day for a week:

1. Drink 1 glass of water before your morning coffee
2. Carry your water bottle everywhere you go
3. Pause and hydrate before responding to stress

Watch how your body begins to respond with renewed clarity, strength, and grace.

Make It Work for You

You don't need hours in the gym, fancy equipment, or a picture-perfect routine to care for your body well, you just need intention. What matters most isn't how long or how intense your wellness habits are. It's about showing up with consistency, grace, and a willingness to make it work for your life, not someone else's.

Let go of the all-or-nothing thinking. Wellness isn't about rigid checklists or chasing unrealistic goals. It's about finding rhythms that fit your season, your schedule, and your soul. When you stop trying to squeeze your life into someone else's routine and instead invite God into your own, everything shifts. There is peace, purpose, and progress, even in the smallest steps.

Commit to the Lord whatever you do, and He will establish your plans.
—Proverbs 16:3, NIV

Rhythm Over Routine: Instead of aiming for "perfect," aim for "possible."

Try this:

1. Wake up and stretch for five minutes before you reach for your phone. Let your body feel gratitude before the world rushes in.
2. Walk after dinner as a family wind-down or solo worship time. Movement + prayer = healing in motion.
3. Prep lunch while listening to a sermon, podcast, or scripture audio. You'll nourish your body and your spirit at the same time.
4. Turn chores into cardio. Put on worship music while vacuuming, scrubbing, or folding laundry, and let joy fill the room.
5. Combine connection with wellness. Have a phone call with a friend while walking laps around the block.

Remember: These small movements, small shifts, and small choices compound over time. Ten intentional minutes a day can add up to over an hour a week. That's progress. That's stewardship. That's honoring the temple God has given you.

Coach Strategy: Habit Stacking That Fits Your Life

Habit stacking is a simple and powerful tool. Just add a small wellness habit onto something you're already doing:

After brushing your teeth ⇨ 10 squats

After making your coffee ⇨ drink a full glass of water

After reading your Bible ⇨ do 5 minutes of stretching

After putting the kids to bed ⇨ take a calming walk or do deep breathing

The key is to tie wellness to what already exists in your life. That way, you don't have to create time, you just have to honor it differently.

Grace-Filled Encouragement

Sweet sister, God sees how much you carry. The invisible labor. The constant giving. The sleepless nights and selfless love. That's why your wellness journey must serve you, not enslave you. It's not about checking another box. It's about saying yes to the strength, peace, and vitality that allow you to show up fully for the people you love.

You are allowed to start small. You are allowed to modify. You are allowed to change your mind. But you are not allowed to give up on yourself. You don't need hours. You need intention. You don't need perfection. You need patience with yourself. And every small, faithful step counts.

Stay Encouraged and Accountable

Consistency isn't built in isolation, it's strengthened in community, When the motivation dips (and it will), encouragement and accountability are the bridges that carry you across.

This journey toward honoring your body with grace isn't meant to be walked alone. Start with something simple: write it down. When you journal your intentions, emotions, and wins, no matter how small, you create a record of your growth. These pages become evidence that you're showing up, even when it's hard.

Then, share it with someone safe. Find a wellness partner: a friend, sister, cousin, or another mom who's also committed to becoming her healthiest self. Start a simple text thread. Swap encouragement. Share your wins. Cheer each other on.

Try these accountability prompts:

- What made you feel strong today?
- What did you do today that honored your body or mind?
- Where did you choose grace over guilt?
- What small win are you celebrating this week?
- How can I pray for you in your wellness journey this week?

You'll be amazed at how healing it is just to be seen, heard, and celebrated by someone else walking a similar road.

You can also create *a Wellness Celebration Jar.* Every time you make a healthy choice: drinking water instead of soda, going for a walk instead of scrolling, choosing sleep over stress. Write it on a slip of paper and add it to the jar. On a tough day, pull one out and remind yourself: You are doing better than you think.

Coach Tip: Your wellness isn't just about habits. It's about hope. Surround yourself with people who speak life over your progress, not shame over your pace.

Let Go to Move Forward

Sometimes, the most transformative health decision isn't to add something, but to release what's weighing you down. True wellness isn't just about exercise or nutrition; **it's also about freedom.** Emotional, mental, and spiritual freedom.

We often carry invisible burdens: guilt for missing workouts, shame for emotional eating, comparison to other women who "seem to have it all together," or impossible standards we set for ourselves. These aren't motivators. They're chains. Sis, you were never meant to live shackled by the "shoulds."

Let us throw off everything that hinders and the sin that so easily entangles. And let us run with perseverance the race marked out for us. —Hebrews 12:1, NIV

Letting go is not giving up. It's surrendering control to the One who knows the deepest desires of your heart and the healthiest pace for your journey.

Ask yourself:

1. What health or body shame story am I still believing?
2. What expectation or rule am I holding onto that's draining my joy?
3. What can I release this week to make room for rest, energy, or peace?

Maybe it's:

- Letting go of perfection in your meal planning
- Releasing guilt for taking a rest day
- Forgiving yourself for "falling off" again and simply starting fresh
- Saying no to a diet or trend that steals your joy and feels heavy

Coach Tip:

Write it down on a sticky note or a slip of paper (whatever you're releasing) and physically throw it away, burn it *safely,* or tear it up as an act of surrender. Sometimes your body needs to feel the freedom you're choosing.

Letting go isn't weakness. It's wisdom. It's saying, "I trust God's grace more than my grind." And that's where true strength and healing begin.

Connect It to Legacy

Your health is not just about how you look. It's about how you live. It's about the moments you want to be fully present for, the laughter around the dinner table, the vacations you dream of taking, the ministry you feel called to lead, and the legacy of love, energy, and wholeness you want to pass on to your children and grandchildren.

When you choose wellness, you're not being selfish. You're sowing seeds of generational strength. Your daughter is watching how you speak to yourself in the mirror. Your son is watching how you treat your body and prioritize your time. And whether you realize it or not, you are teaching them what it looks like to steward a life with joy, purpose, and self-respect.

> *The righteous lead blameless lives; blessed are their children after them.*
> —*Proverbs 20:7, NIV*

I remember a day that still lingers in my heart like a quiet whisper. I had taken my children to the playground with good intentions. But as I tried to keep up with them, I found myself gasping for breath, too winded to run, too weary to engage. I watched them laugh and play while I sat on the bench pretending to scroll my phone, hiding my exhaustion and silently grieving the energy I no longer had. That moment crushed me. Not because

I wasn't "fit," but because I wasn't free. My body had become a barrier to presence. That realization broke something open within me.

I didn't want my kids to remember a tired, overwhelmed mom always too drained to play. I wanted them to remember a mama who chased them across fields, danced in the living room, and showed up to life with joy in her eyes and strength in her stride.

That day was a divine invitation. Not to hustle harder or chase perfection, but to heal. To rebuild my energy, one step at a time. To restore the vessel God gave me. And to begin living in a way that honored the legacy I longed to leave. Your legacy is not just what you leave behind; it's also what you create. It's what you live right now.

Your health matters not just for the sake of your lifespan, but for your lifeforce: the energy and spirit you bring into every room, every hug, every bedtime story, every sermon, every project. When you care for your body, you multiply your capacity for love, laughter, purpose, and impact.

So sweet sister, if you've ever felt like you were too tired to be the woman you were created to be, know that change is possible. And it doesn't have to be drastic. It just has to be intentional. You don't need to climb a mountain tomorrow. But maybe today, you walk around the block. You refill your water bottle. You stretch. You breathe. You rest. You begin again.

Legacy doesn't start someday. It starts now. With how you love your body. How you honor your energy. How you show up for you.

What would it look like to live your life like your grandchildren are already watching? What would it mean to run toward your calling without being slowed down by exhaustion or disconnection? Choose vibrancy. Choose strength. Choose stewardship. Choose life, and leave a legacy that echoes for generations.

One Loving Commitment at a Time

Transformation doesn't begin with a gym membership or a fridge overhaul. It begins with a decision. A moment of love. One tiny, intentional "yes" to yourself.

Too often, we set ourselves up with unrealistic expectations, imagining that true health means waking up tomorrow with a perfect routine, perfectly planned meals, and endless motivation. But the truth is: you don't need to do everything at once. You just need to do one thing today, one small act of love that honors the beautiful, purpose-filled vessel God has given you.

It might be pouring a glass of water instead of soda. It might be stepping outside for a five-minute prayer walk. It might be going to bed 30 minutes earlier instead of scrolling. It might even be pausing to breathe, stretch, and say, "Thank you, God, for this body."

These aren't insignificant steps, they're seeds. Seeds of healing. Seeds of self-respect. Seeds of legacy. And over time, when planted consistently in grace and love, they grow into rhythms that can sustain your joy, your calling, and your energy for years to come.

Do not despise these small beginnings, for the Lord rejoices to see the work begin.
—*Zechariah 4:10, NLT*

This isn't a race to perfection. It's a return to wholeness. It's choosing to believe that every moment of nourishment, movement, hydration, and rest is not just physical, it's spiritual stewardship. You were bought at a price. You are worthy now. And you are capable of loving yourself into strength, not punishment.

So don't wait for a Monday. Don't wait for motivation. Just choose one loving commitment today. A promise that says, "I matter." A promise that reflects how deeply God values you.

Today's Journal Prompt:

Today, I will take care of my body by _____ because I love myself and I honor God with my health.

Let that be your start. Then tomorrow, choose again. Grace upon grace. Glory to glory. Step by step. Love by love. And remember: You don't need to get it all right, you just need to stay rooted in love. That's the kind of progress that heaven celebrates.

Applying the GRACE Method to Your Physical Health

☐ **G: Ground Yourself in God's Truth:** Your body is not your enemy, it's a temple. You were fearfully and wonderfully made (Psalm 139:14), and God delights in how you care for what He created.

☐ **R: Reflect on Your Current Reality:** What is your energy like right now? Are you exhausted, depleted, and ignoring your own needs? Be honest, not harsh. Where can you give yourself more love?

☐ **A: Act with Intentional Steps:** Pick one habit to start this week: movement, hydration, sleep, or nourishment. Keep it simple. Keep it sacred.

☐ **C: Create Consistent Systems:** Set a routine: Meal prep Sundays. Walk after lunch. Bedtime rituals. These rhythms become your anchor.

☐ **E: Embrace Progress Over Perfection:** You don't need a perfect fitness journey. You need a faithful one. Progress counts. Rest counts. Grace counts.

Reflection Questions

1. What is one small step I can take this week to care for my body?
2. What is my current relationship with rest, movement, or nourishment?
3. How does taking care of my body help me walk in my purpose?
4. What lies have I believed about my body that God wants to replace with truth?

A Prayer for Physical Health

Heavenly Father,

Thank You for the body You have entrusted me with. Forgive me for the times I have neglected or criticized this sacred vessel. Teach me to honor You by honoring my health. Help me to move with joy, nourish myself with love, and rest with intention. Let every step I take be an act of worship. I release perfectionism and invite Your grace into my wellness journey. Strengthen me to steward my health well, so I can live, love, and serve with vibrancy. Thank You for dwelling within me. I choose to honor that gift today.

In Jesus' name, Amen.

Disclaimer: The content in this chapter (and throughout this book) is for informational and inspirational purposes only and is not intended as a substitute for professional medical advice, diagnosis, or treatment. Always consult your physician or qualified healthcare provider before beginning any new health, nutrition, fitness, or wellness regimen. The author and The Real Life Series Publishing Co., LLC dis-

claim any liability for injuries, losses, or damages incurred as a result of following the content presented herein. Your health decisions should always be made in partnership with your full medical team.

WEEKLY WELLNESS REFLECTION WORKSHEET

Do you not know that your body is a temple of the Holy Spirit...?
— 1 Corinthians 6:19

Reflect on Your Week:

1. How did I honor my body this week?

_____
_____
_____

2. What movement made me feel joyful or strong?

_____
_____

3. What nourishing choices did I make that I'm proud of?

_____
_____

4. Did I get enough rest and recovery? Why or why not?

_____
_____

5. What challenged me this week in caring for my body?

_____
_____

6. What helped me stay on track (or get back on track)?

_____
_____

My Progress:

☐ I drank enough water on most days
☐ I moved my body at least 3 times
☐ I ate meals that fueled me instead of draining me
☐ I rested when needed
☐ I stayed aware of God's presence in my body-care journey

Looking Ahead:

One wellness intention for the week ahead:

This week, I will _____

Because I deserve to feel _____

QUICK AND JOYFUL MEAL IDEAS FOR BUSY MOMS

Meals designed to be nourishing, satisfying, and realistic for your full life. These meals are meant to be guilt-free, grace-filled, and fuel for your purpose:

BREAKFAST: 5-Minute Morning Wins

- **Power Smoothie:** Blend almond milk, frozen berries, banana, spinach, and protein powder.
- **Greek Yogurt Parfait:** Layer Greek yogurt with granola, honey, and fruit.
- **Avocado Toast with Egg:** Whole grain toast + smashed avocado + sprinkle of sea salt + fried or boiled egg.
- **Overnight Oats** (Make the night before): Rolled oats + almond milk + chia seeds + cinnamon + berries in a mason jar.
- **Nut Butter Banana Wrap:** Whole wheat tortilla + almond or peanut butter + banana + cinnamon—roll it up and go.

LUNCH: Nourishing in 10 Minutes or Less

- **Build-Your-Own Salad Bowl:** Prewashed greens + protein (rotisserie chicken, tuna, boiled eggs) + veggies + nuts + vinaigrette.
- **Leftovers Remix Wrap:** Yesterday's dinner + whole grain wrap + fresh spinach or slaw mix.
- **Protein-Packed Snack Plate:** Hummus, cheese cubes, boiled egg, cherry tomatoes, almonds, apple slices, whole grain crackers.
- **Simple Soup & Side:** Heat up a low-sodium soup + serve with avocado toast or a mini salad.
- **Turkey or Veggie Burger Lettuce Wraps:** Skip the bun, add a dollop of mustard or hummus, and wrap in romaine leaves.

DINNER: 15–20 Minute Favorites

- **Sheet Pan Chicken & Veggies:** Toss diced chicken, broccoli, carrots, and potatoes with olive oil + seasoning. Bake at 425°F for 20 minutes.
- **Stir-Fry in a Flash:** Frozen veggie mix + pre-cooked chicken or shrimp + low-sodium soy sauce + brown rice.
- **Taco Tuesday (Any Day):** Ground turkey, black beans, taco seasoning, whole wheat tortillas, and a toppings bar.
- **One-Pot Pasta with Spinach and Garlic:** Whole wheat pasta + olive oil + garlic + baby spinach + parmesan = comfort + fuel.
- **Breakfast for Dinner:** Scrambled eggs + fruit + whole grain waffles or toast + turkey sausage.

BONUS: Healthy Snack Ideas

- Apple slices with almond butter
- Baby carrots and hummus
- Trail mix (nuts, seeds, dark chocolate chips)
- Boiled eggs and grapes
- Cottage cheese with pineapple

WELLNESS IN 5 MINUTES: A QUICK START GUIDE FOR BUSY WOMEN

Even five minutes can reset your body, mind, and spirit. Use this cheat sheet when time is tight but your well-being matters.

1. 5-Minute Movement

- Stretch your arms, back, and legs
- Do 10 squats, 10 jumping jacks, 10 wall push-ups
- Dance to one uplifting or worship song
- Walk briskly around your home or outside

Coach Tip: Movement energizes your mood, don't wait for motivation. Start, and momentum will follow.

2. 5-Minute Prayer or Stillness

- Sit quietly and breathe deeply: Inhale for 4, hold for 4, exhale for 8
- Meditate on a scripture (e.g., Psalm 46:10 "Be still, and know that I am God...")
- Pray for your body, your mind, your day, and your family

Faith Anchor: "Draw near to God and He will draw near to you." — James 4:8

3. 5-Minute Nourishment

- Drink a full glass of water (bonus: add lemon or fruit)
- Prep a smoothie, protein snack, or overnight oats
- Eat a fruit or veggie snack (e.g., apple + peanut butter, carrots + hummus)

Fuel Reminder: You're not just feeding your body, you're fueling your purpose.

4. 5-Minute Hydration Reset

- Refill your water bottle
- Add ice and a fruit slice for freshness
- Sip slowly while saying an affirmation: "I honor my body as God's temple. I care for it with love."

5. 5-Minute Reflection or Planning

- Journal: "How can I honor my health today?"
- Write your top 1–2 wellness intentions for the day
- Review your schedule and find one 10-minute slot for movement

Legacy Tip: One small shift today plants seeds for a healthier tomorrow.

Final Encouragement:

Sis, five minutes of wellness is still wellness. These small acts are not insignificant; they are crucial. And you are worthy of care, no matter how busy life gets.

Mini Routine Guide: Simple Rhythms for a Stronger You

You don't need hours or perfection, just a rhythm that honors your season. Use this guide to gently build physical, spiritual, and emotional strength each day.

Morning Reset (10–15 Minutes)
Purpose: Set the tone with God, movement, and hydration.

- Wake & Hydrate: Drink a full glass of water before anything else.
- Ground in the Word: Read one verse + speak one affirmation. Suggested: 1 Corinthians 6:19 or Proverbs 31:17
- Stretch or Move: 5–10 minutes of gentle movement (walk, stretches, or dance)
- Intention Check: "What's one way I will care for my body today?"

Midday Boost (10 Minutes)
Purpose: Realign your energy and mindset

- Move Your Body: Walk for 5–10 minutes (even inside the house)
- Hydrate: Refill your water bottle and take deep breaths
- Refocus: Listen to 5 minutes of worship, an uplifting podcast, or pray

Evening Wind Down (10–15 Minutes)

Purpose: Reflect, release stress, and prepare to restore
- Wellness Journal Prompt: "What did I do today to honor my body?" "Where did I show myself grace?"
- Light Nourishment: Herbal tea or a nourishing evening snack.
- Stretch & Breathe: Gentle movements to relax.
- Bedtime Prayer: Thank God for your body, breath, and the progress you've made.

Weekly Wellness Rhythm at a Glance: (Day and Focus, Example)

1. Movement Monday: 10-minute dance break or family walk
2. Try It Tuesday: New healthy recipe or water goal
3. Wednesday Wellness Check-In: Track how you feel and adjust goals
4. Thankful Thursday: Gratitude walk or prayer for your health
5. Flex Friday: Gentle yoga or stretch session
6. Self-Care Saturday: Extra hydration, journaling, or a nap
7. Sunday, Sabbath & Soul Reset: Full rest, reflection, and soul nourishment

Empowerment Reminder:

You are not lazy. You are not behind. You are building a new rhythm rooted in love, not shame. Let these mini moments become holy habits of healing.

CHAPTER 17

Financial Health: Stewardship and Stability

The financial guidance in this chapter is provided for informational, inspirational, and educational purposes only. It is not a substitute for professional financial, legal, or tax advice. Please consult with a licensed financial advisor or professional before making any financial decisions. Your unique situation matters.

Faith, Freedom & Fruitfulness

> *The wise store up choice food and olive oil, but fools gulp theirs down.*
> — *Proverbs 21:20, NIV*

Money is not your enemy. Misalignment is. Financial peace isn't just about dollar signs; it's about stewardship. It's about obedience. It's about making intentional choices so that your money serves your God-given mission, not the other way around.

Proverbs 21:20 paints a clear contrast between wisdom and waste. The wise person saves, plans, and builds with foresight. The foolish one consumes everything in the moment, leaving nothing for the future. This isn't just about budgeting; it's about honoring God with the way we prepare, prioritize, and provide for others.

I know what it feels like to stretch a single meal across nine plates with more faith than food in the pantry. I've stared at bills I couldn't pay, tears in my eyes, and prayers on my lips. And yet, I've also given when it didn't make sense, tithed when it felt impossible, and watched God show up with supernatural provision and favor. Every act of faith was matched with His faithfulness.

Financial wellness is not just about spreadsheets and savings goals; it's a spiritual posture. It's trusting that you're not alone in this, and it's never too late to make a shift.

You are not behind. You are not unworthy of abundance. You are not broke or broken. You just have to look at what remains, what you have left, and put it in God's hands to bless and multiply.

You are being called into a new season of wisdom, strategy, and overflow, one prayer, one plan, one brave financial decision at a time. Let's walk it together, with grace and expectancy.

1. Your Money Mindset: What Do You Believe?

Let's begin at the root: What did you grow up believing about money? Maybe you heard things like, "Money doesn't grow on trees," or "We can't afford that." Perhaps you were taught that wealthy people are selfish, or that wanting more was somehow unspiritual. Or perhaps your family struggled so deeply with lack that today, you find it hard to release anything. You save everything "just in case," and giving feels risky instead of joyful.

The truth is this: money is not evil, and it is not your identity. It's a tool, a neutral resource that reflects your heart and priorities. In Matthew 6:21, Jesus says, "For where your treasure is, there your heart will be also." Money doesn't define who you are, but it does show your priorities and what matters to you.

The Bible never condemns wealth, only the love of it. "For the love of money is the root of all kinds of evil..." (1 Timothy 6:10). The problem isn't money; it's misplaced worship. When money becomes your master, you serve it. But when money becomes your servant, you use it to glorify God.

Let's look at **How Scripture Defines the Purpose of Money:**

Provision: "And my God will liberally supply (fill until full) your every need according to His riches in glory in Christ Jesus." — Philippians 4:19, AMP

Stewardship: "In this case, moreover, it is required [as essential and demanded] of stewards that one be found faithful and trustworthy." — 1 Corinthians 4:2, AMP

Generosity: "You will be enriched in every way so that you may be generous, and this [generosity, administered] through us is producing thanksgiving to God [from those who benefit]." — 2 Corinthians 9:11, AMP

Wisdom: "The plans of the diligent lead surely to abundance and advantage, But everyone who acts in haste comes surely to poverty." — Proverbs 21:5, AMP

Money isn't meant to be worshiped, feared, or ignored. It's intended to be wisely managed, generously shared, and joyfully stewarded for kingdom purposes.

God doesn't just want you to "get by." He wants to teach you how to thrive, heart first, then wallet. He cares about every bill, every bank account, and every budget line because He cares about your peace.

Beloved, I pray that you may prosper in all things and be in health, just as your soul prospers. —*3 John 1:2, NKJV*

Money Reflection Prompt

Take a moment to journal your answers:

1. What are three beliefs I currently carry about money?
2. Which ones are helping me walk in wisdom and freedom?
3. Which ones are rooted in fear, shame, or scarcity that I may need to release to God?

2. Stewardship Over Striving

Let's talk about the difference between striving and stewarding, because they don't produce the same fruit. Striving is rooted in pressure and performance. It says, "If I hustle harder, I'll have enough. If I prove my worth, I'll finally feel secure." It often leads to burnout, comparison, and discontent.

Stewardship, on the other hand, is *rooted in trust and wisdom.* It says, "God, everything I have is from You, and I want to honor You with it, whether it's a little or a lot." You don't need a six-figure salary to be a good steward. You need a surrendered heart and a willing spirit.

Jesus said, "Whoever can be trusted with very little can also be trusted with much..." (Luke 16:10, NIV). That means the way you manage $100 matters just as much as the way you would manage $10,000. God isn't just watching the size of your income; He's watching the faithfulness of your choices.

Stewardship is:

- Saying "no" to impulse spending so you can say "yes" to your future peace.
- Choosing to tithe, even when it stretches you, because you trust God more than your math.
- Making a plan for your money instead of wondering where it all went.
- Remembering that every dollar has an assignment, and you are the manager, not the slave.

Let's stop waiting for "when I make more" to start honoring God with our finances. Peace doesn't come with more money. Peace comes with greater clarity, purpose, and alignment with God's will and way.

Empowerment Tip

Budgeting is not about restriction; it's about intention. Your budget is not a punishment. It's your blueprint for peace. It's the practical plan that helps your values show up in your spending. It's where you tell your money, "You're going to serve God's purpose in my life."

Stewardship Reflection Prompt

1. Where am I striving in my finances instead of stewarding?
2. Is my spending aligned with my values, or with my emotions?
3. What is one simple change I can make this week to reflect wiser stewardship?

3. Practical Peace: Know Where It's Going, A Budget That Works for Real Life

Let's take a deep breath together, friend. Money doesn't have to feel overwhelming. One of the most empowering things you can do for your peace, your purpose, and your household is to know exactly where your money is going. Because guess what? Financial chaos thrives in secrecy, but peace begins with clarity.

A budget isn't a punishment. It's a mirror and a map. It reflects what matters most to you and helps you navigate your way to financial peace and provision.

A budget that works is one that's honest. Not based on the numbers we wish we made or the expenses we pretend don't exist, but one that takes into account your real income, your real needs, and your real dreams. No shame. No fluff. Just truth and grace.

Let's simplify the process with a proven starting point: *the 50/30/20 Rule.* This is a helpful framework that gives every dollar a job and brings structure to your spending:

The 50/30/20 Budget Breakdown:

50% for Needs: Essentials that keep your life functioning: rent/mortgage, utilities, groceries, insurance, gas, and minimum payments on debts.

30% for Wants: These are the things that add joy and comfort: meals out, travel, beauty appointments, streaming services, or birthday gifts. These aren't wrong; they just need boundaries.

20% for Financial Goals: This is where peace grows. Think giving, tithing, savings, building your emergency fund, paying off debt faster, investing, or setting aside money for that dream God placed on your heart.

Practical Tip: Adjust the ratios to reflect your real life.

If your needs currently eat up more than 50%, give yourself grace, but use this framework as a goal to work toward. Even if you can't put 20% toward sowing and savings right now, starting with 2% is still beneficial. It's not about perfection; it's about progress.

Try This: Use a Monthly Budget Worksheet (printable or digital) to break down your income and expenses by category.

Start by listing:
- Total income (after taxes)
- Fixed expenses (same every month)
- Variable expenses (can change each month)
- Debt payments (minimum + any extra)
- Savings contributions
- Tithing and generosity

- "Miscellaneous" (because life always brings the unexpected)

Budgeting Affirmation:

"I am not behind. I am building. Every dollar I track is a step toward peace, provision, and purpose. I am worthy of financial clarity and security."

Reflection Questions:

1. Do I know where every dollar is going, or am I guessing?
2. What part of budgeting feels most overwhelming to me?
3. How would my life feel different if I had a plan for my money each month?

4. Break Free from Debt, With Grace and Grit

Let's start with truth: Debt does not define you. It doesn't mean you're irresponsible. It doesn't mean you're too late. And it certainly doesn't mean you're a failure.

Debt is often the result of real-life moments: emergencies, survival, student loans, helping loved ones, or simply not having the financial tools you needed at the time. So take a deep breath, let go of shame, and pick up something far more powerful: grace-filled grit and a willingness to grow.

You are not stuck. You are starting. And every wise financial step you take is evidence that you're reclaiming your peace and walking toward freedom.

Your Debt Freedom Plan:

Step 1: List Every Debt Honestly, Write down each account with the following details:

- Total Balance:
- Minimum Monthly Payment:
- Interest Rate:
- Due Date:

Being honest with what you owe is the first step toward taking back control. Don't be afraid of the number; facing it means you're already on your way out. Focus on and remember that you are more than a conqueror, in life and over debt as well (Romans 8:37).

Step 2: Choose Your Payoff Strategy

The Debt Snowball:

☐ Focus on the smallest balance first (regardless of interest).
☐ Make minimum payments on everything else.
☐ Throw any extra dollars at that small balance.
☐ When it's paid off, roll that payment into the next debt.

This builds quick wins and emotional momentum.

The Debt Avalanche

☐ Focus on the highest interest rate first.
☐ Save more money over time on interest.
☐ Best for long-term savings and disciplined planners.

Empowerment Tip: Neither method is "better". Choose the one that fits your mindset and motivation style. Momentum matters more than method.

Step 3: Commit to Consistency, Not Perfection

Even $20 extra a month toward your debt matters. Every payment is a declaration:

"I am not powerless. I am not stuck. I am building a legacy of freedom."

Set a calendar reminder. Automate payments if possible. Track your progress and celebrate every milestone, no matter how small.

Biblical Encouragement:

The rich rule over the poor, and the borrower is slave to the lender.
— *Proverbs 22:7, NIV*

This verse isn't meant to shame you. It's a reminder that debt can keep us in bondage, but God's desire is for us to walk in freedom, stewardship, and peace.

Debt-Freedom Affirmation:

"I am not what I owe. I am who God says I am. I release shame, ask for, and step into strategy. With grace and grit, I will walk in financial freedom."

Reflection Questions:

1. What feelings do I associate with my debt, and where do I need healing?
2. Which debt payoff strategy (snowball or avalanche) feels most sustainable for me?
3. What's one small step I can take this week to reduce my debt load?

5. Build an Emergency Fund: Start Where You Are

Life doesn't give us a heads-up. The car breaks down. The fridge stops working. A child spikes a fever the night before payday. Emergencies don't wait for a "convenient" moment, and that's precisely why building an emergency fund is one of the most powerful acts of financial self-care you can take.

But here's the key: start where you are, not where you think you "should" be. An emergency fund isn't about fear; it's about freedom. It's not about hoarding, it's about having margin. When life throws the unexpected your way, your emergency fund stands between you and stress, anxiety, or unnecessary debt.

The Two-Phase Emergency Fund Plan:

Phase One: The Starter Fund: Aim for $500 to $1,000

This is your fast-access, peace-of-mind fund for urgent needs, such as car repair, medical copays, or a sudden job shift. Keep it in a separate savings account to avoid accidental spending.

Phase Two: The Long-Term Buffer: Build toward 3–6 months of essential living expenses (rent/mortgage, utilities, food, insurance, gas, etc.)

This protects you from job loss, major medical emergencies, or other life disruptions, and gives you time to breathe and make wise decisions under pressure.

Empowerment Tip: Don't be discouraged by small beginnings. Every dollar is a seed of peace. Whether you set aside $5, $50, or a windfall like a tax return, you're building protection for your future self.

Creative Ways to Start Saving:

1. Set up automatic transfers of $10 to $25 per paycheck.
2. Sell unused items in your home (clothes, gadgets, décor).
3. Save unexpected money: birthday gifts, refunds, bonuses, and side gig cash.
4. Cut one "want" a week (e.g., coffee runs or takeout) and stash the savings.

Scripture Inspiration:

> *The wise store up choice food and olive oil, but fools gulp theirs down.*
> *— Proverbs 21:20, NIV*

Again, this verse reminds us that wise people plan ahead, preserving and preparing, not out of fear, but out of wisdom and stewardship. Building an emergency fund is a biblical act of foresight.

Emergency Fund Affirmation:

"I may not have it all today, but I have what I need to begin. Each dollar saved is

a declaration of wisdom, trust, and preparation. I am creating margin for peace."
Reflection Questions:

1. What would financial peace look and feel like in my life right now?
2. What is one small sacrifice I can make each week to start saving for emergencies?
3. How can I turn unexpected income into a seed for future security?

6. Multiply Your Income with Creativity and Courage

You were never meant to live in a state of lack. And you certainly weren't created to stay stuck. Inside of you (*yes, you*) are God-given gifts, creative ideas, and talents that can be activated for impact and income. Whether you're trying to pay off debt, build an emergency fund, or create financial breathing room, it starts by seeing yourself as capable and called.

You don't need to wait for the "perfect" job or a once-in-a-lifetime opportunity. You can start with what you already have, right here, right now. A little courage. A little creativity. And a whole lot of faith.

Now to Him who is able to {carry out His purpose and} do superabundantly more than all that we dare ask or think {infinitely beyond our greatest prayers, hopes, or dreams}, according to His power that is at work within us...
— *Ephesians 3:20, AMP*

The Power of Permission

Sometimes the most significant barrier to earning more isn't a lack of resources; it's the belief that you're not allowed to pursue them. Hear this from me, sister to sister: It's not selfish to desire overflow. It's stewardship. Overflow will enable you to give more, stress less, and walk in your calling with freedom, rather than fear.

Let's give ourselves permission to build income without guilt, and without apologizing for wanting better.

Creative Income Expansion Ideas:

Here are just a few of the ways women like you are earning income in the margins of busy lives:

- **Freelance Services:** writing, proofreading, social media management, design, virtual assistant support.
- **Sell Digital Products:** planners, checklists, homeschool resources, devotionals, templates.
- **Launch a Coaching or Service Business:** life coaching, faith-based mentoring, meal prep services, organizing, or decluttering help.
- **Teach or Host:** lead a local workshop, a Bible study with a workbook, or offer an online mini-course.
- **Use What You Have:** rent out a room, your car, or equipment through peer-to-peer platforms.
- **Leverage Your Lifestyle:** babysitting, tutoring, hair braiding, dog walking, laundry folding, or making freezer meals for other moms.

You don't need to do all of them. Just pick one that excites you, and start small. Is there one or two that sparked your interest or spoke to your spirit? Did anything spark a possible new creative idea that you can begin to execute?

Income Brainstorming Exercise

Grab a journal or notepad and write down your answers to the following:

1. What do people already come to me for help with?
2. What skills or hobbies do I enjoy that could serve someone else?
3. If I had to earn an extra $100 this month, how could I do it?

Now, list 10 ideas. Don't overthink it. Don't edit yourself. Just list them. Then, circle one and try it this month. Even if it doesn't lead to a big payday, you'll build momentum and confidence. And that's worth more than you know.

Courageous Action Step

Put a date on your calendar to try one of your ideas within the next 7 days. Tell a friend for accountability. And pray this over your effort:

"Lord, use what I have in my hands. Bless it. Multiply it. And let it serve others and glorify You."

Biblical Wisdom on Increase

Give, and it will be given to you. A good measure, pressed down, shaken together and running over, will be poured into your lap. For with the measure you use, it will be measured to you. — Luke 6:38, NIV

She considers a field and buys it; out of her earnings she plants a vineyard. — Proverbs 31:16, NIV

The virtuous woman in Proverbs 31 wasn't just nurturing; she was entrepreneurial. She saw opportunities. She made investments. She wasn't afraid to multiply what she had, and neither should you.

Affirmation for Abundance:

"I am creative, capable, and called. God provides not just enough, but more than enough. I will multiply what I have in my hands with wisdom and faith."

7. Give Generously, Even Now

You don't need to wait until you're wealthy to be generous. Giving isn't about a number; it's about the posture of your heart. Whether you have much or little, there's something powerful that happens when you open your hand instead of clenching your fist. When you give, especially when it stretches you, you're declaring to God (and to yourself) that your trust is in Him, not your bank balance. And trust me, God always honors trust.

Honor the Lord with your wealth, with the firstfruits of all your crops. — Proverbs 3:9, NIV

Each of you should give what you have decided in your heart to give, not reluctantly or under compulsion, for God loves a cheerful giver. — 2 Corinthians 9:7, NIV

Giving Is a Spiritual Strategy

In God's economy, giving is never a loss; it's an act of obedience that opens the door to supernatural provision.

You're not just giving to a person, church, or cause. You're sowing seeds into eternity. You're partnering with God to meet needs, shift atmospheres, and bring heaven to earth. Your life becomes an avenue or way for God's Kingdom to come and His will to be done on earth as it is in Heaven. And that harvest? It often returns to you in ways you can't even measure: peace, clarity, provision, and open doors.

I've given when I didn't know how I'd make the grocery budget work. I've tithed when it would've made more "sense" to save. And I've seen God take my small obedience and turn it into overflow. Not overnight. But on time, every time.

Start Small. Be Consistent.

Giving isn't about waiting until you "have enough." It's about choosing to believe that God is your Source, even now. Start where you are.

- Give a tithe (10% of your income).
- Start with a set amount weekly or monthly that stretches you but doesn't stress you. Make sure you are giving with a cheerful heart, not with resentment in your heart and mind.
- Give your time, encouragement, or meals if money is tight. Generosity isn't limited to finances.

Let each one give {thoughtfully and with purpose} just as he has decided in his heart, not grudgingly or under compulsion, for God loves a cheerful giver {and delights in the one whose heart is in his gift}. —2 Corinthians 9:7, AMP

Give, and it will be given to you. A good measure, pressed down, shaken together and running over, will be poured into your lap. For with the measure you use, it will be measured to you. — Luke 6:38, NIV

Empowerment Tip: Create a Giving Line in Your Budget

Whether it's $5 or $500, make generosity part of your financial rhythm. Build it into your budget as a non-negotiable. Don't wait for the "extra." Invite God into your finances by putting Him first.

Sample Budget Line Ideas:
- Giving/Tithe – 10% (or any higher committed percentage)
- Blessing Others Fund – $20/month (to buy a coffee, send flowers, or bless someone anonymously)

The Heart of a Giver, Ask yourself:

1. What do I feel God nudging me to give, even if it feels small?
2. Who in my life might need encouragement, support, or generosity this week?
3. Where can I make space in my budget to be a blessing?

Encouraging Affirmation:

"I give joyfully and faithfully. God multiplies my obedience. I trust Him as my Source, and I give as an act of love, worship, and purpose."

8. Teach Financial Legacy to the Next Generation

Your children are watching how you manage money. Are you modeling fear or faith? Chaos or clarity?

Teach Them This:

- ☐ Set savings goals (with jars or apps)
- ☐ Let them earn and give
- ☐ Show them how you plan meals, budget, and tithe.
- ☐ Talk about needs vs. wants.

This isn't just about numbers. It's about breaking cycles and creating legacy.

Final Encouragement

Sis, I know money can feel heavy. But God never meant for it to be a burden. He calls you to freedom, not fear. He equips you to be the head and not the tail. He's calling and equipping you to operate at a higher level. And He promises wisdom to those who ask.

So start where you are, with what you have, and let faith lead the way. You are not behind. You are not too late. You are being positioned to thrive financially, to steward well, and to bless others richly.

Remember: Wealth is not just for consumption. It's for contribution. And your money, in God's hands, becomes ministry.

Applying the GRACE Method:

☐ **G: Ground Yourself in God's Truth:** You are not defined by your bank account. You are a steward, not an owner. God is your Source.

☐ **R: Reflect on Your Current Reality:** Where are you financially right now? What habits are serving you, or sabotaging you?

☐ **A: Act with Intentional Steps:** Create your budget. Choose a debt payoff method. Build your emergency fund. Try a new income stream.

☐ **C: Create Consistent Systems:** Schedule a weekly money check-in. Use worksheets. Set monthly financial goals.

☐ **E: Embrace Progress Over Perfection:** Celebrate every win. Forgive every slip. Keep moving forward, one faithful dollar at a time.

Reflection Questions

1. What financial habit has helped, or hurt, your peace the most?
2. What would financial freedom allow you to do more of?
3. What's one step you can take this week toward greater stewardship?

Prayer for Financial Wholeness

Father God,

Thank You for being my ultimate Provider. I surrender every fear, every burden, and every decision about money to You. Teach me to be a wise steward. Help me to live with integrity, generosity, and peace. Break every cycle of lack or fear in my family line. Show me how to honor You with every dollar, every investment, every act of giving. I trust You to multiply what

I offer and to lead me into overflow, not just for myself, but so I can bless others and so everyone around me can have everything they need.

In Jesus' name, Amen.

Disclaimer: The financial content in this chapter (and throughout this book) is provided for informational and educational purposes only and is not intended as financial, investment, legal, or accounting advice. Readers are encouraged to consult with a licensed financial advisor, tax professional, or attorney before making any financial decisions or implementing any strategies discussed in this book.

The author and The Real Life Series Publishing Co., LLC do not assume any responsibility or liability for any loss or damages incurred as a result of the use of the information provided. All financial decisions should be made based on individual circumstances, goals, and professional guidance. Use of this content is at your own discretion and risk.

CHAPTER 18

Order, Organization & Physical Environment

Creating Sacred Spaces for Life to Flourish

Let all things be done decently and in order. — *1 Corinthians 14:40, KJV*

I used to believe that organized women were born with a special gene. The ones whose pantries looked like Pinterest boards, who always knew where their kids' shoes were, and who somehow managed to fold laundry before it turned into Mount Neverrest. Then one morning, after stepping on yet another toy and realizing I couldn't even find my favorite water bottle, I knew it was time for a change. Not perfection. Not aesthetics. Peace.

Creating a well-ordered environment is one of the most loving things you can do for your mental, emotional, and spiritual well-being. It's not about having the cleanest house on the block or impressing guests. It's about building a sanctuary that serves your soul, reflects your purpose, and supports your family.

Let's start by assessing where we are, not to judge ourselves but to create a new foundation.

Your Organization Assessment

Take a deep breath: This is a Judgment-Free Zone. Let's start by naming what's true, not to shame you but to set you free.

Sometimes, disorganization isn't about laziness or lack of discipline; it's about survival. It's the result of carrying too much for too long. It's what happens when you're tending to everyone else's needs while silently drowning in your own. And if you've ever looked around your space and felt defeated before the day even began, sis, you're not alone.

This is your time to pause for a gentle check-in. Not to label you, but to lovingly guide you toward the life and peace you deserve.

Ask Yourself:

1. How often do you misplace essentials, such as your keys, phone, wallet, or charger?

☐ Every day?
☐ A couple of times a week?
☐ Occasionally?
☐ Almost never?

2. How do you feel when you walk into your main living space?

☐ Calm and centered?
☐ Distracted and drained?
☐ Energized and motivated?
☐ Overwhelmed and on edge?

3. When guests are on their way, what's your first reaction?

☐ "We're ready!"
☐ "I need 10 minutes to tidy."
☐ "Let's just meet at their place instead."

4. How many 'clutter zones' do you have that consistently pile up?

☐ Entryway?
☐ Kitchen counter?
☐ Dining table?
☐ That one chair in your room? (You know the one.)

5. Do you have routines in place that help maintain peace in your home?

☐ Morning and evening resets?
☐ A system for papers, mail, or school forms?
☐ Designated drop zones for keys, bags, or shoes?

6. Emotionally, how does your home make you feel right now?

☐ Safe and restful?
☐ Claustrophobic and cluttered?
☐ Neutral?
☐ A little bit chaotic?

If your space could speak, what would it say about you?

☐ "She's in survival mode."
☐ "She's trying her best."
☐ "She's creating peace, one drawer at a time."
☐ "She's an organizing expert."

Why This Matters

The goal here isn't to check boxes. It's to raise awareness. Because when you know what's weighing you down, you can start making space for what lifts you up.

Your space reflects your season, and sometimes your pain. However, it can also reflect your progress, peace, and purpose. Even if things feel out of control right now, please hear this: You are not failing. You are simply ready for a fresh start.

Try This: Start a simple **"Peace Check" Journal.** Each day, jot down:

•   One area that triggered stress:

•   One small win (even if it was just clearing the sink):

•   One action you'll take tomorrow to move forward.:

It's not about fixing your whole life overnight. It's about taking one gentle, loving step toward a space that supports your healing, your family, and your God-given purpose.

The Seven-Step Framework for Home Organization:

1. Grace-Based Decluttering: Less Stuff, More Peace

Let's begin not with shame, but with grace. This is not about having a perfect home. It's about creating a space that allows you to breathe, think, worship, rest, and be the woman God called you to be. You don't need a label maker and a whole weekend to make progress. You need one moment of permission to begin. Because when your home feels heavy, your heart often does too.

Let's lighten the load, not to impress anyone, but to set ourselves free. This is grace-based decluttering, not a chore, but a spiritual invitation to remove what no longer serves your peace or purpose.

We start with what we already have. No shopping required. No over-hauls necessary. Just honest evaluation, loving intention, and one faithful step at a time.

Use the Grace-Filled Four-Box Method:

As you go through your space, keep it simple and spirit-led. Label four containers (or just four piles on the floor) with the following:

1. **Keep:** These are the things you love, use often, or need for your current season. They add value or joy. They help you function or reflect your faith.

2. **Donate:** These are items that are still in good condition but no longer serve your life or style, such as clothes, kitchen tools, books, or toys that could bring joy to someone else. Let them go joyfully.

3. **Trash:** Broken things, expired items, single socks waiting on a miracle. Thank God for the experience they provided and toss them. Releasing clutter isn't wasteful; it's worshipful when it frees your mind and your home.

4. **Relocate:** Sometimes, things just need to go back to their rightful place. A toy in the kitchen, a mug in the bedroom, a jacket in the hallway, return them to where they belong.

Don't Try to Declutter Everything Today

Please hear me: You do not have to tackle the whole house. This is a process, not a performance. Start small. One drawer. One shelf. One basket of mail. Choose one place that's been silently stressing you out and give it your loving attention for just 10 or 15 minutes.

Put on worship music. Light a candle. Inhale deeply and remind yourself: *"I'm not behind. I'm building peace, one decision at a time."*

Coaching Insight:

Decluttering isn't about removing stuff; it's about making room. Room to breathe. Room to hear God clearly. Room for rest. Room for the woman you're becoming. This isn't minimalism. This is intentional living. This is stewardship. This is self-love. This is spiritual maturity in action.

2. Room-by-Room Systems: Creating Spaces That Serve Your Life

You don't need to reorganize your entire house in one weekend. That's not grace; that's burnout in disguise. Instead, let's take it one space at a time, weaving peace into your home through purpose and love. Each room can be transformed into a place that supports your calling, your rhythms, and your well-being.

This is not about impressing guests; it's about **restoring the woman who lives here.** Let's walk through your home together, room by room, with grace in our hands and peace as our goal. These are just suggestions as everyone's home and daily life experience is different.

Kitchen: Nourishment + Flow

This is the heart of your home. It's where meals are made, prayers are whispered over the stove, and life unfolds between sips of coffee and clattering dishes.

Week 1: Clear the Counters + Set the Tone
- ☐ Remove everything from the countertops.
- ☐ Only place back what is used daily.
- ☐ Designate a Landing Zone near the door for keys, mail, or backpacks. This small act alone can eliminate daily stress.

Week 2: Declutter the Pantry with Purpose
- ☐ Group similar items: baking goods, snacks, canned items.
- ☐ Toss expired products.
- ☐ Use bins or clear containers if possible as it helps you see what you have and stop overbuying.
- ☐ Add a small whiteboard or notepad to keep track of staples running low.

Week 3: Create Functional Drawers
- ☐ Assign each drawer a purpose: utensils, meal prep tools, food storage, etc.
- ☐ Use organizers or small baskets.
- ☐ If you open a drawer and it overwhelms you, it's time to simplify.

* *And this is true for other areas of your life as well. If it overwhelms you, it might be time to simplify)*

Empowerment Tip: Add one special item, a candle, scripture card, or plant, to remind you that even everyday tasks can be sacred.

Living Room: Connection + Calm

This is where connection lives. Whether it's movie nights, quiet reading, or heart-to-hearts with your kids, this space should support rest and relationship, not chaos.

Refresh Flat Surfaces
- ☐ Clear coffee tables and side tables.
- ☐ Keep only what you use or love, a couple of books, a cozy throw, a tray for remotes.

Create Home for Essentials
- ☐ Use a small basket for remotes.
- ☐ Designate a space for shared items like games, books, or devotional tools.

Coaching Wisdom: Visual clutter creates mental clutter. Create space that says "You're safe here."

Bedroom: Sanctuary for Your Soul

Your bedroom should feel like a deep breath, not a dumping ground.

Declutter What Doesn't Promote Rest
☐ Remove laundry piles, paperwork, and anything work-related.
☐ Keep surfaces minimal: a lamp, a journal, a framed prayer or affirmation.

Create a Gentle Morning + Evening Routine
☐ Morning: Make the bed, open the curtains, speak a declaration (*"Today is a day of purpose and peace."*)
☐ Evening: Light a candle, stretch, pray, prep for tomorrow.

Empowerment Tip: You don't have to have a fancy bedroom to feel rested. You just need to be intentional.

Children's Rooms: Ownership + Order

This is the perfect opportunity to invite your children into the peace-building process.

Involve Them in Decluttering
☐ Ask: "What toys or clothes do you no longer use?"
☐ Use color-coded bins or picture labels so they can maintain their systems.

Create Simple Habits They Can Follow
☐ Toy rotation: put some items away and swap them every few weeks.
☐ Establish a clean-up routine before bedtime.

Let them decorate a small "quiet corner" with books or faith-based affirmations.

Mom-to-Mom Encouragement: It doesn't have to be perfect. It just needs to be teachable. You're planting seeds of stewardship.

Bathroom: Refresh + Renew

This is often the first place you start your day. Let's make it work for you, not against you.

Declutter with Mercy
- ☐ Toss expired medications, half-used hotel shampoos, or broken hair tools.
- ☐ Keep daily items accessible, and less-used items tucked away.

Group Like with Like
- ☐ Skincare together. Hair tools together. First-aid in one spot.
- ☐ Use trays, cups, or bins to separate categories.

Empowerment Tip: Place a sticky note on your mirror with a verse or affirmation. Let it greet you before your to-do list does.

Laundry Room: Simplify the Cycle

Laundry can feel never-ending, but the goal here is not perfection, it's peaceful progress. Let's simplify the system so it serves your life, not steals from it.

Make the Flow Make Sense
- ☐ Keep a hamper for each family member or type of laundry (e.g., lights, darks, towels).
- ☐ Store detergent, dryer sheets, and stain removers in a basket or bin within reach.
- ☐ Hang a small rod or install hooks for air-dry items or prepped out fits.

Create a Rhythm, Not a Rush
- ☐ Try themed days: "Towel Tuesday" or "Sheets Saturday."
- ☐ Start and complete one load per day: wash, dry, fold, and put away.

Empowerment Tip: Decorate your laundry room in a way that makes you want to spend time there. Add a small sign that says, *"Serving with love, one load at a time."* Let this space be a place of quiet faithfulness, not frustration.

Entryway: Peace Begins at the Door

This is the first thing you see when you enter and the last thing when you leave. Let it speak peace, not panic.

Set Up a Landing Zone
- [ ] Add a basket, shelf, or wall hooks for keys, bags, and coats.
- [ ] Place a shoe tray or small rug for easy slip-off and clean-up.
- [ ] Include a catch-all bowl or bin for mail, receipts, or sunglasses.

Give Everything a Home
- [ ] If kids toss backpacks on the floor, give them a cubby or a hook at their level.
- [ ] Rotate seasonal items: hats and gloves in winter, sunscreen and shades in summer.

Empowerment Tip: Add a message board with a rotating verse, blessing, or reminder: "You are loved. You are equipped. You've got this."

Home Office or Workspace: Clear Desk, Clear Mind

Whether it's a full room, a corner in the kitchen, or a tiny desk in the bedroom, your workspace should feel focused and faith-filled.

Declutter for Clarity
- [ ] Remove non-work-related items that distract or overwhelm.
- [ ] Keep only what you need within arm's reach: laptop, pens, notebook, planner.

Create Zones
- [ ] Zone 1: Work essentials (laptop, phone, planner)
- [ ] Zone 2: Reference materials (books, files)
- [ ] Zone 3: Inspiration (a photo, scripture, quote)

Add Sacred Touches

☐ Keep a prayer journal nearby.
☐ Use a diffuser or candle to help you reset.
☐ Consider a "Start and End" ritual. Pray before you begin and again when you close the laptop.

Empowerment Tip: Write a sticky note with this affirmation: *"This is divine work. I show up with faith and focus."*

Car Organization: Peace on the Go

Your car is a moving sanctuary. Let's set it up to support the beautiful chaos of life: drives to work, school drop-offs, grocery runs, and everything in between.

Declutter Weekly
☐ Keep a small trash bag, reusable trash can, or tote inside.
☐ Remove food wrappers, receipts, and extra cups regularly.

Create Emergency Kits
☐ Glove box: Registration, insurance, pen, notepad.
☐ Back seat/trunk: Umbrella, extra water, mini first-aid kit, wipes, tissues, and snacks.
☐ For kids: A bin with books, quiet toys, headphones, or devotion cards.

Add Calming Elements
☐ A soft worship playlist.
☐ A verse card on the dashboard: *The Lord watches over you, the Lord is your shade at your right hand; – Psalm 121:5*
☐ A car diffuser with lavender or citrus oil for peace and alertness.

Empowerment Tip: Speak peace over your car (and over yourself) each morning: "God, go before me and make every crooked place straight."

3. **Accessible Storage Solutions:** Make It Easy to Find, Easy to Maintain

Beautiful organization isn't about perfect pantries or buying fancy containers you can't afford. It's about creating systems that serve your life, not stress it. Real-life organization should be functional, accessible, and grace-filled, especially for busy moms, wives, or women navigating full plates. Let's make it easier to keep things tidy and peaceful by making your storage simple, smart, and sustainable.

Use Clear Bins and Jars (Visibility = Peace):

This isn't for everyone, but for many, being able to see what you have is less likely to lead to overbuying, underuse, or feeling overwhelmed. Use clear plastic bins for pantry items, bath essentials, or seasonal clothes. Re-purpose glass jars for dry goods, hair accessories, or small office supplies. Labeling them adds clarity, but the transparency itself gives you instant awareness and peace.

Label Everything (Make It Obvious, Not Fancy):

Labels aren't just for looks. They're loving instructions for your future self (and your family). When everything has a name and a home, it takes the guesswork and the mess out of daily life. Use removable labels, chalkboard tags, or even painter's tape and a marker. This isn't about perfection; it's about communication and calm.

Store Daily-Use Items at Eye Level (Make Life Easy):

Don't tuck the most-used things in hard-to-reach places. Keep your everyday essentials, such as your favorite mug, kids' lunch containers, or devotional journal, within easy reach. Think of eye-level shelves and front-of-the-fridge spaces as prime real estate. If it's something you use every day, make it easy to access without stress or strain.

Repurpose What You Already Have (Stewardship Over Spending):

You don't need to break the bank to create peace. Look around your home: old baskets can corral socks, mason jars can hold bathroom supplies, and shoeboxes can become drawer dividers. Get creative and resourceful.

This isn't about trendy products; it's about wise stewardship. God can multiply what you already have when you use it with purpose.

Coaching Tip: The "One-Step Rule":

If it takes more than one step to put something away, it's too complicated. Streamline your systems so even the littlest hands in your home can help. No lids on toy bins. No top-shelf-only baskets for daily-use snacks. Keep it simple so it stays sustainable. Peace thrives in spaces that are easy to maintain, not just aesthetically pleasing.

You don't need to have the "perfect" system. You just need one that works for you. Your home is a living, breathing space, and your storage solutions should adapt and evolve as your life changes with the seasons.

Simple steps:
- ☐ Use clear bins or jars
- ☐ Label everything
- ☐ Store daily-use items at eye level.
- ☐ Repurpose what you have to save money.

4. Create Sustainable Routines: Rhythms That Ground You in Grace

Life is full. And when you're juggling work, kids, ministry, meals, appointments, and maybe even trying to drink enough water, routines can feel like just one more thing to figure out. But here's what I've learned: Sustainable routines are not about perfection. They're about peace. They're about building rhythms that support your soul, not systems that shame you when you miss a step.

Think of routines as gentle anchors that hold your day steady, not rigid rules that weigh you down. When done with intention and grace, even the simplest habits can create a calm and clear atmosphere in your home.

Morning Reset: Start with Light and Intention
Before the rush, before the emails, before the "Mom, I can't find my shoes!" Take a moment to ground yourself. Not in hustle, but in peace.

☐ *Make the bed:* It's a small win that signals to your brain: "We're starting fresh."

☐ *Open the blinds:* Let the light in. Natural light can lift your mood and shift your mindset.

☐ *Tidy one space:* Whether it's clearing your nightstand or wiping the bathroom counter, one small tidy spot creates momentum.

Coach's Tip: Say a short prayer as you make your bed. Something like, "Lord, help me create peace in every space I step into today." Or simply, "Holy Spirit, have your way today, In Jesus' Name, Amen."

Evening Reset: Release the Day, Prepare for Peace

Evening routines are your invitation to exhale. To create closure. To reset the room and your spirit, for tomorrow.

☐ *Clean the dishes:* Nothing steals joy like waking up to yesterday's mess.

☐ *10-minute pickup:* Set a timer, turn on some music, and let everyone pitch in. Quick tidy-ups prevent chaos from piling up.

☐ *Prepare for tomorrow:* Pack lunches, lay out clothes, and glance at the calendar. Future-you will thank you.

Coach's Tip: Light a candle or play soft worship music while you clean. Turn this into sacred time, not just chores.

Weekly Reset: A Rhythm of Renewal

Instead of trying to "do it all" daily, give yourself one day to refresh and refocus for the week ahead.

☐ *Meal plan:* Just jot down 3–4 simple dinners. Don't overcomplicate it.

☐ *Deep clean one room and rotate it every week.* Today, the bathroom; next week, the kitchen. Progress, not perfection. Perform quick wipe-downs and clean-up sessions between deep cleanings.

☐ *Update your calendar:* Sync your week with your values. Prioritize peace over packed schedules.

Coach's Tip: Use this time to reflect. Ask yourself, "What's one thing I can simplify this week to create more peace in my home?"

Why This Matters

When you set rhythms that reflect your season of life and honor your capacity, you're not just organizing your home; you're nurturing your heart. Sustainable routines make room for joy. For stillness. For focus. And they remind you that peace isn't found in control, but in consistency. Let it be simple. Let it be soulful. Let it be filled with grace.

- *Morning Reset:* Make the bed, open the blinds, and tidy one space.
- *Evening Reset:* Clean dishes, 10-minute pickup, prep for tomorrow.
- *Weekly Reset:* Meal plan, deep clean one room, update calendar.

5. Family Participation: Making Peace a Shared Priority

Sweet friend, let me remind you of something beautiful: you were never meant to carry it all alone. Yes, you're strong. Yes, you're capable. But God designed the family unit to function as a team, each member playing a vital role in creating a home that reflects love, order, and grace. When you shift from doing everything yourself to inviting your family into the process, you're not just managing a house; you're building a legacy.

Involve Every Age Group (Yes, Even the Little Ones)

Everyone can contribute, no matter how small their hands may be. Teaching responsibility and stewardship isn't just about clean floors or folded laundry. It's about raising children who understand the value of service, community, and care.

Age-Appropriate Task Ideas:

- *Ages 2–4:* Put toys in bins, throw away trash, carry laundry to the basket, wipe spills with a small cloth.

- *Ages 5–8:* Make their beds, match socks, set and clear the table, feed pets, and organize school bags.
- *Ages 9–12:* Sort and fold laundry, clean their room, load/unload dishwasher, vacuum, manage chore charts.
- *Teens:* Do their own laundry, meal prep, babysit siblings, organize family calendar, and lead cleanup after dinner.

Coach's Tip: Use encouraging phrases like "You're such a helper!" or "Thank you for bringing peace to our home." Words plant seeds that grow into confidence.

Host Monthly Family Meetings (Make It Fun!)

Family meetings don't have to be stiff or awkward. Think of them as a team huddle where everyone gets a voice.

Keep it simple:

- ☐ Choose a time when everyone is home (pizza night works great!).
- ☐ Go around and ask: What's working well? What's been frustrating?
- ☐ Review the calendar together to identify any upcoming busy weeks.
- ☐ Adjust chore rotations or routines as needed.
- ☐ End with a gratitude round or a short family prayer.

Coach's Tip: Keep meetings under 20 minutes. Give everyone a job (note-taker, snack bringer, timekeeper) so it feels like a team, not a lecture.

Celebrate Small Wins Together

Did your five-year-old finally remember to put her shoes in the basket without being asked? Celebrate that! Did your teenager help with meal prep or vacuum the car? Praise that effort!

Celebration builds connection. When you recognize the small victories, you cultivate a culture of encouragement rather than criticism.

- ☐ Create a "Family Win Board" or a sticker chart just for fun.
- ☐ Plan a reward, such as a game night, homemade dessert, or movie

night, when a goal is met.
- ☐ Speak life: "You're doing such a great job being part of this home. I'm so proud of you."

Coach's Tip: Say this aloud often: *"We're not just cleaning a house, we're building a peaceful life together."*

Why This Matters

When you lead with love and invite your family into the process, you teach them more than routines, you teach them how to love well, how to serve with joy, and how to contribute to peace in shared spaces. You model grace, not perfection. And that is the heart of a thriving home.

Simple Strategies:
- ☐ Involve every age group with age-appropriate tasks
- ☐ Hold monthly family meetings to adjust systems.
- ☐ Celebrate small wins together.

6. Seasonal Organization Strategies: Flow with the Seasons, Not Against Them

Just like nature moves through seasons of bloom, rest, harvest, and preparation, so do we. Your home doesn't have to be in a constant state of perfection. It simply needs to reflect your current season, serve your family's needs, and leave room for grace.

Each season of the year brings its own energy and challenges. When you take time to organize with the seasons in mind, you'll find more peace, more margin, and more flow, not more to-do lists. Let's break it down by season:

Spring: Declutter and Deep Clean

Spring is a season of renewal. The air is lighter, the sun is brighter, and it's the perfect time to refresh your home and your spirit.

Focus Areas:
- ☐ Let go of what no longer serves you: clothes, paper piles, winter

gear.
- ☐ Open the windows and invite in fresh air and fresh perspective.
- ☐ Deep clean one room each week (or one drawer each day).
- ☐ Donate items you didn't use this winter.

Coaching Encouragement: Spring cleaning isn't about being spotless; it's about making space for what's growing. What in your life is trying to bloom, but is crowded by clutter?

Try This: *"Spring Peace List":*
What 3 spaces would bring the most relief if they were decluttered this season?

Summer: Simplify & Adjust the Rhythm

Summer is often full of movement, vacations, kids at home, late sunsets. With everyone's schedule a little different, organization becomes less about structure and more about flexibility and simplicity.

Focus Areas:
- ☐ Set up easy-to-grab stations for sunscreen, swimsuits, towels, and outdoor toys
- ☐ Declutter backpacks, lunch boxes, and school items no longer in use
- ☐ Create a family "summer bin" for outings (snacks, wipes, water bottles, first aid)
- ☐ Adjust daily routines to accommodate relaxed bedtimes or travel

Coaching Encouragement: In this season, less is more. Make your systems simple enough to maintain while you're on-the-go or soaking in slow mornings.

Try This: Create a *"Summer Rhythm Chart"* with flexible routines: morning reset, afternoon downtime, evening wind-down, even 15 minutes of "daily joy."

Fall: Prepare for School, Structure, and Sacred Rhythms
Fall brings with it a return to routine, school, sports, and work sched-

ules. It's a sacred time to re-anchor the family and create systems that support your next level.

Focus Areas:
- ☐ Prep closets: donate outgrown clothes, organize uniforms, jackets, and shoes.
- ☐ Set up a *Family Command Center* with calendar, mail sorter, and school papers.
- ☐ Stock up on grab-and-go lunch items, breakfast staples, and meal plans.
- ☐ Refresh your daily routines: morning launches, after-school reset, bedtime rhythm.

Coaching Encouragement: Fall is a season of harvest. What habits or routines are you planting now that will reap peace in the coming months?

Try This: Host a *"Back-to-Routine Reset Day"* let the whole family get involved in prepping their spaces and setting shared expectations.

Winter: Simplify, Reflect, and Reset

Winter invites stillness. It's a time for cozy, for quiet, for less hustle and more heart. Don't fight the slower pace, lean into it.

Focus Areas:
- ☐ Declutter holiday decor, wrapping supplies, and gift items post-holiday
- ☐ Create cozy zones with blankets, books, candles, and warm lighting
- ☐ Prep spaces for snow gear or indoor activities
- ☐ Reflect on what worked this year and what needs to shift in the new year

Coaching Encouragement: You don't have to do everything right now. Winter is a time to exhale, reset, and nurture what matters most.

Try This: *"Winter Reset Reflection"*:
- What area of your home or life needs a gentle reset?
- What do you want more of in this next season?

Final Word of Encouragement

Be encouraged no matter what the state of your environment is. You are in a season, and seasons aren't meant to be rushed. They're meant to be honored. Let your home evolve with you. Let your systems bend with your season. Let go of guilt and lean into grace. Organizing your home isn't about control, it's about care.

Simple Strategies:

- Spring: Declutter and deep clean
- Summer: Organize outdoor gear and adjust schedules
- Fall: Prepare for school and holidays
- Winter: Simplify and reset for the new year

7. Purpose-Driven Space Inspiration

Writing or Dreaming Space

Set up a cozy corner with a notebook, candle, and vision board. Keep inspiring quotes or scriptures nearby. Let it be a place where ideas and dreams feel safe to be born.

Prayer or Reflection Space

Carve out a quiet nook, even if it's just a chair by the window or a closet with twinkle lights. Add your Bible, a journal, a blanket, and a "do not disturb" moment in your day.

Kitchen With Purpose

Organize your kitchen so that nourishing your family feels joyful, not stressful. Prep your space for meal planning, prayer over meals, and even creative moments with your kids.

Bedroom Sanctuary

Remove chaos and clutter. Dim the lighting. Add soft textures. Make it a place where your soul can exhale. Let your bed be a symbol of rest, not a holding place for laundry and to-do lists.

Office or Business Corner

Even a small desk can hold big vision. Keep your tools in reach, clutter away, and inspiration in view. Whether you're running a business or launching an idea, create a space that honors your excellence.

Empowerment Tip: Your Home Is a Ministry, Not a Museum

Friend, your home doesn't need to be showroom-ready. It's not meant to impress strangers. It's meant to serve your soul and welcome *your people.* It's a living space, not a proving space. And it becomes sacred the moment you say, *"God, use this space for Your glory."*

- Let the laughter in your living room be louder than your insecurities.
- Let your kitchen carry the aroma of love, not stress.
- Let your prayer corner be a portal to peace, not perfection.
- Let your children's clutter remind you of life being lived, not a mess to be judged.

Try This: Room-by-Room Vision Exercise

In your journal, write down:

"In this space, I want to feel _____. I want it to help me _____. To support that, I will remove _____ and add _____."

Then go room by room this week, just one at a time, and begin to align each area of your home with the kind of life you're creating.

Final Thought

Your environment should support your emotional health, not sabotage it. It should nurture your faith, not distract it. And it should echo the truth of who you are becoming, not just who you've been.

Let your home become a declaration of healing, joy, clarity, and divine purpose. You are building a space that holds not only your belongings, but your becoming.

Applying the GRACE Method:

- ☐ **Ground Yourself in God's truth:** 1 Corinthians 14:33 reminds us that God is a God of order, and we are made in His image (Genesis 1:27). Therefore, our environments should reflect that truth.
- ☐ **Reflect on your current reality:** What space is draining your peace?
- ☐ **Act with intention:** Choose one small area to focus on and reset.
- ☐ **Create consistent systems:** Create your morning and evening routines and rhythm.
- ☐ **Embrace progress over perfection:** Celebrate one small win to-day.

Reflection Questions:

1. What space in your home feels most overwhelming, and why?
2. How does your physical environment affect your emotional and spiritual health?
3. What one habit could you start this week to bring more peace into your home?

Prayer Over Your Environment:

Father,

Thank You for being a God of order and peace. Help me create a home that reflects Your presence, love, and purpose. Teach me to let go of what no longer serves this season of life, and show me how to steward my space with wisdom, grace, and joy. May every drawer I open and every corner I tidy be a sacred act of faith. Breathe new life into my home and into my heart. In Jesus' name, Amen.

Sis, you don't have to be perfect. You just have to start. One drawer. One habit. One heart-led decision at a time. You've got this. And I'm right here cheering you on.

CHECKLIST AND JOURNAL REFLECTION QUESTIONS FOR EACH ROOM

Laundry Room

Checklist:

- ☐ Sort laundry hampers by person or category (e.g., lights, darks, towels).
- ☐ Store detergents and cleaning supplies in labeled bins or baskets.
- ☐ Install hooks or a rod for hanging clothes to air-dry.
- ☐ Establish a consistent laundry rhythm (e.g., one load per day).
- ☐ Add an inspiring quote or sign to bring warmth to the space.

Journal & Reflection Questions:

1. What part of the laundry routine feels most stressful to me, and why?
2. How could I reframe laundry as an act of service and care?
3. What one change could make this process easier or more enjoyable?

Entryway

Checklist:

- ☐ Create a designated landing zone for keys, bags, and shoes.
- ☐ Add a bin or tray for mail and other daily carry items.
- ☐ Rotate seasonal items (e.g., umbrellas, gloves, sunscreen).
- ☐ Install child-height hooks or cubbies for backpacks or coats.
- ☐ Add a family message board or verse card at the entrance.

Journal & Reflection Questions:

1. How do I feel when I walk into my home?
2. What is the first message I want my family or guests to receive here?
3. What could I remove or rearrange to bring more peace to this area?

Home Office

Checklist:

- ☐ Clear your desk of non-essential or distracting items.
- ☐ Set up zones for essentials, references, and inspiration.
- ☐ Keep your workspace tidy with organizers or trays.
- ☐ Add faith-based or calming items (e.g., diffuser, prayer journal).
- ☐ Begin and end your work time with prayer or a blessing.

Journal & Reflection Questions:

1. Does my workspace reflect the work God has called me to do?
2. What distractions can I eliminate to improve my focus?
3. How can I infuse more peace and inspiration into my workday?

Car

Checklist:

- ☐ Declutter the car weekly: remove trash, papers, and unused items.
- ☐ Organize the glove box and trunk with labeled kits or pouches.
- ☐ Create emergency kits that include health essentials, snacks, and weather-related items.
- ☐ Add a calming scent or diffuser to your car interior.
- ☐ Play peaceful or worship music to set the tone for your day.

Journal & Reflection Questions:

1. What do I typically feel during car time: stress, peace, distraction?

2. How can I use car time for prayer, worship, or stillness?
3. What simple routine could make my drive feel more peaceful and purposeful?

SHOPPING YOUR HOUSE FOR STORAGE SOLUTIONS

A No-Spend Guide to Getting Organized with What You Already Own

Before you click "add to cart," take a walk around your home to shop your home first. Chances are, you already have everything you need to create beautiful, functional storage systems.

STEP-BY-STEP PLAN

Step 1: Reframe Your Mindset

Instead of thinking, "I need to buy bins," start asking, "What can I reuse, repurpose, or relocate to make this space work better for me?"

Step 2: Identify Storage Needs by Room

Write down what items need homes. Example: mail, toys, socks, snacks, pens, cleaning supplies.

Step 3: Tour Your Home

Go through each room and look for unused or underused containers, baskets, tins, jars, boxes, trays, or bins.

Step 4: Match What You Find With What You Need

Get creative. A cute mug can hold pens. A shoe box becomes a drawer divider. That old diaper caddy? Now it's for cleaning supplies.

Step 5: Personalize & Beautify

Add labels. Line boxes with wrapping paper. Use leftover contact paper.

Even a repurposed container deserves to be cute!

WORKSHEET: SHOP YOUR HOUSE INVENTORY

Storage Need:

Items to Organize:

Repurposed Solution Found in Home:

Room to Use It In:

Notes / To-Do:

Example:
Mail Sorting
Incoming/outgoing bills, notes
Wooden tray from the coffee table
Kitchen landing zone
Add label "Mail"

QUICK IDEAS FOR WHAT TO REPURPOSE

Found Around the House: Can Be Used For...

- **Mason jars or glass jars:** for pens, dry goods, cotton balls, and snacks

- **Shoe boxes:** for drawer dividers, bathroom storage

- **Baskets:** for toys, blankets, and pantry grouping

- **Mugs:** for makeup brushes, pens, scissors

- **Trays or lids:** for entryway catch-alls, jewelry displays

- **Over-the-door hooks:** for bag or towel storage in small spaces

- **Tupperware without lids:** for sock drawer organizers, toy bins

- **Diaper caddies or totes:** for cleaning supplies, homework stations

Reflection Questions

1. What surprised you about what you already had?
2. How did it feel to repurpose instead of purchase?
3. What space in your home now feels more peaceful?
4. What's one creative storage solution you're proud of?
5. What will you organize next with what you already own?

Purpose-Driven Room Planner: A guided worksheet to help you create sacred spaces that reflect who you are and support the woman you're becoming.

> *By wisdom a house is built, and through understanding it is established; through knowledge its rooms are filled with rare and beautiful treasures.*
> — *Proverbs 24:3–4, NIV*

Instructions: Use this worksheet to journal through each room in your home. There is no pressure to fill everything at once. Start with the space that calls to your spirit, and return as often as needed. One room, one shift, one step at a time.

ROOM NAME: _____
(Example: Kitchen, Bedroom, Entryway, Prayer Corner, etc.)

1. Current Feelings - When I walk into this room, I feel:

☐ Peaceful
☐ Overwhelmed
☐ Distracted
☐ Inspired
☐ Tired
☐ Other: _____

2. Vision Statement

In this space, I want to feel: _____
This room should help me: _____

3. Purpose Check-In: What is this room primarily used for?

☐ Rest & Renewal
☐ Connection & Community
☐ Creativity & Productivity
☐ Worship & Prayer
☐ Nourishment
☐ Family Life
☐ Other: _____

4. What's Not Working?

List 2–3 things in this space that don't align with your vision or values:

_____
_____

5. What Can I Let Go Of? (Items, furniture, decor, clutter, distractions, or even guilt!)

_____
_____
_____

6. What Can I Add or Rearrange to Reflect My Purpose?
(List textures, scents, colors, systems, lighting, spiritual touches, etc.)

_____

_____

_____

7. Small Next Step: What is ONE small thing I can do this week to bring this space closer to my vision?

*   *Repeat this process for as many rooms or corners as needed. You don't need to do it all today. Progress over perfection. Peace over pressure.*

BONUS EMPOWERMENT DECLARATION:

"This room is no longer just a space; it's a sanctuary for the life I'm building, the peace I'm claiming, and the purpose I'm pursuing. I bless this space to reflect God's goodness in me and around me."

CHAPTER 19

Leisure, Fun & Sites to See: Joy is Holy Too

Joy Isn't Extra, It's Essential

A cheerful heart is good medicine, but a crushed spirit dries up the bones.
— *Proverbs 17:22, NIV.*

Let me ask you something that might make you squirm a little: When was the last time you had fun? Not the kind where you're organizing everyone else's enjoyment, not the "fun" that comes after you've crossed off every item on your to-do list, but real, soul-stirring, belly-laughing, lose-track-of-time kind of fun?

If you're sitting there trying to remember, you're not alone. If you're feeling a twinge of guilt just thinking about prioritizing your own joy, welcome to the club that no woman should have to join...the *"I Don't Deserve Fun Until Everyone Else Is Happy"* society.

Here's what I've learned after years of coaching women who've forgotten how to play: The enemy doesn't just steal your peace, he steals your joy. And when he steals your joy, he steals your strength.

The Permission You've Been Waiting For

Let me be the first to tell you what your heart needs to hear: Joy is not selfish. Joy is spiritual. You are not being a bad mother when you laugh until your sides hurt. You're not being an irresponsible wife when you take time to do something purely because it brings you delight. You're not being a poor steward when you invest in experiences that refresh your soul.

You are being obedient to a God who created you not just to work and serve, but to live abundantly, and abundance includes joy, wonder, and delight.

The thief comes only in order to steal and kill and destroy. I came that they may have and enjoy life, and have it in abundance {to the full, till it overflows}.
—John 10:10, AMP

The Joy Crisis No One Talks About

There's a silent epidemic in our lives, and it's called *Joy Poverty*. It's sneaky, quiet, and socially accepted. No one gasps when a woman says she hasn't done anything for herself in months. In fact, we often reward that kind of self-neglect with applause. "She's so selfless," they say. But deep inside, that kind of constant giving without receiving can lead to soul erosion.

Joy Poverty happens when we spend so much time managing, mothering, serving, performing, or pleasing others that we forget we're allowed (called, even) to experience joy ourselves. It's when our own delight falls to the very bottom of the priority list... or disappears altogether.

The Biblical Root of Joy: A Spiritual Birthright

Joy is not a bonus. It's not extra. It's not a luxury reserved for when your home is spotless, your work is caught up, and your kids are thriving. Joy is a fruit of the Spirit (Galatians 5:22), a supernatural byproduct of life with God. It's an anchor for our hope (Hebrews 6:19), a strengthener for our spirit (Nehemiah 8:10), and a reflection of God's own character (Zephaniah 3:17).

You weren't just saved to survive, you were saved to thrive. When you starve yourself of joy in the name of responsibility, you're not becoming holier; you're simply becoming more hollow. This can result in a profound and painful experience of numbness, detachment, or a lack of purpose. This can manifest in various ways, impacting both your mental and physical well-being. So make sure you take steps regularly to let your life be filled with joy,

But the fruit of the Spirit {the result of His presence within us} is love {unselfish concern for others}, joy, {inner} peace, patience {not the ability to wait, but how we act while waiting}, kindness, goodness, faithfulness —Galatians 5:22, AMP

...And do not be worried, for the joy of the Lord is your strength and your stronghold. —Nehemiah 8:10, AMP

Signs You Might Be Living in Joy Poverty:

Let's name the symptoms, because awareness brings healing: (check the symptoms you may be feeling).

- ☐ You feel guilty anytime you're not "productive."
- ☐ You can't recall the last time you did something simply because it made you smile.
- ☐ You only rest or relax if it serves someone else ("I'll feel better when...")
- ☐ You feel anxious when you're not in motion.
- ☐ You've lost connection with what you actually enjoy.

Sound familiar? That's not just burnout; it's a form of bondage. It's a sign that the enemy has convinced you that your joy is optional. But Jesus didn't say, "I came that they may have life and have it orderly." He said, "I came that they may have life and have it abundantly." (John 10:10). God desires that you experience a life filled with spiritual richness. When you intentionally include time with people and engage in activities that bring you joy and fulfillment, and lead a life centered on a relationship with God, you experience a deeper sense of purpose, peace, and love, often manifesting as a positive impact on both yourself and others.

The True Cost of Joy Deprivation:

Let's not sugarcoat it. Living in constant depletion takes a toll:

- Emotional exhaustion and quiet resentment (especially toward those we love most).
- Diminished creativity and vision, we stop dreaming when joy dries up.
- Reduced capacity to serve with love: giving becomes obligatory, not joyful.
- Joyless modeling for our children, who grow up believing adulthood means exhaustion.
- A distorted version of faith that says God only blesses busy women.

The Breakthrough You've Been Waiting For

But here's the breakthrough:

The joy of the Lord is your strength. — Nehemiah 8:10

Let that settle in for a moment. Really hear it. It doesn't say, "The joy of the Lord will be your strength after your to-do list is done." It doesn't say, "The joy of the Lord is your reward for doing everything right." It says the joy of the Lord is your strength. Present tense. Active. Right now. Not later. Not someday. Not after you've earned it or proven yourself worthy.

That means that joy isn't an accessory to your life; it's a necessity. It's not the dessert you get if you've behaved. It's the spiritual nourishment that gives you the strength to endure, to rise, to believe, and to build. It's not optional. It's essential.

Let's be clear: the opposite of joy is not sadness, it's depletion. When joy is missing, you don't just feel down, you feel disconnected…disconnected from your purpose, from your people, and God. Because joy isn't just a feeling, it's fuel. And without it, your soul runs dry.

Let's say it another way: Joy is a weapon. Joy has the power to fight back despair. Joy can silence fear. Joy can rekindle hope in places where grief has long made its home. Joy can restore clarity where confusion once ruled.

You're not weak because you're tired. You're exhausted because you've gone too long without joy. You're not broken, you're burned out. And the remedy is not more hustle. It's more *God-given joy.*

Coach Truth: When joy leaves the room, so does your fire. And a woman without fire cannot light anything: not her family, not her dreams, not her faith.

You can't lead when your joy is limping. You can't nurture others when you've been starved of gladness. You can't chase your calling when your soul is shackled by guilt, fatigue, and the constant need to prove yourself.

But hear me now: It is time, past time, to get your flame back.

That fire? That light? That sparkle in your eyes when you're doing something that makes you feel alive again? That's not just you having a good time; that's you being restored.

That's your strength returning. That's heaven cheering. That's the Holy Spirit breathing fresh wind into your spirit. That's the moment you stop surviving and start living again.

So go on, sis. Light the candles. Play the music. Laugh until your stomach hurts. Do the thing that scares you a little but excites you a lot. Get outside. Paint something. Write something. Dance in your kitchen. Plan the trip. Bake the cake. Try the new hairstyle. Say yes to life again.

Because joy is not a break from your spiritual life; it is your spiritual life. Joy isn't weakness; **it's divine warfare.** It's the sound of chains breaking and freedom rising.

A Blessing Over Your Joy

May the fire of your joy be rekindled. May you remember the girl inside you who loved to laugh and wasn't afraid to play. May you reclaim the woman you are now: powerful, purposeful, and worthy of delight. And may your joy return, not as a fleeting moment, but as the routine and rhythm of your abundant life.

Empowerment Reflections:

Ask yourself:

1. What do I believe about joy?
2. Do I see it as essential or as a luxury?
3. Who taught me that fun must be earned?
4. Whose voices still echo in my decisions today?
5. Am I modeling to my children or community that joy is spiritual, or that it's selfish?
6. What would shift if I made space for joy every day, even in micro-moments?

Practical Next Steps:

Write a Joy Statement: "I believe I am worthy of joy because:

_____

- *Track Your Joy* for one week. Every night, write down one thing that made you smile, even if it was small.
- Reclaim *One Joyful Practice* from your childhood or college years. Do it this week.
- Create a *"No-Guilt Joy List"* of activities that bless you. Post it where you can see it often.

Biblical Power Anchor:

For the Lord your God is living among you. He is a mighty savior. He will take delight in you with gladness. With his love, he will calm all your fears. He will rejoice over you with joyful songs." — Zephaniah 3:17, NLT

God doesn't just tolerate you, He rejoices over you. You're not too broken, too behind, or too busy for joy. You're invited into it.

Reclaiming Your Right to Joy

The Theology of Delight: God didn't create sunsets because they're necessary for survival. He didn't design flowers to smell beautiful because they serve a practical purpose. He didn't give you the capacity for laughter because it's efficient. He created these things, and your ability to enjoy them, because He delights in your delight.

When you experience joy, you're participating in the character of God. When you rest, you're following His pattern. When you play, you're honoring the creativity He placed within you.

Empowerment Truth: Your joy is not frivolous; it's a form of worship. Your laughter is not wasteful; it's a declaration that God is good, even in the midst of life's challenges.

The Joy Audit: Where Do You Stand?

Be honest with yourself as you answer these questions:

Current Joy Assessment: On a scale of 1–10,

- How much joy do you currently experience in your daily life?
- What percentage of your free time is spent on activities that truly bring you delight?
- How often do you engage in activities purely because you enjoy them (not because they benefit others)?
- What stops you from pursuing joy? (Check all that apply):

☐ Guilt
☐ Time
☐ Money
☐ Energy
☐ Family obligations
☐ Feeling undeserving

- What would change in your life if you gave yourself full permission to experience joy regularly?

Leisure, Fun & Local Adventures for Everyday Women

Budget-Friendly Ideas:
- Have a picnic in your local park with your favorite playlist
- A morning walk with a latte in hand
- Attend a free community festival or market
- Try a new library or bookstore for browsing
- Visit a museum on a free-admission day

Creative Fun at Home:
- Host a movie night with popcorn and blankets
- Paint, craft, or create a vision board
- Try a new recipe from a different culture
- Start a puzzle, embroidery, or coloring book

Site-Seeing in Your City:
- Check out botanical gardens
- Visit scenic walking trails or waterfronts
- Explore a neighboring town for a day trip
- Look up historical landmarks or churches in your area

- Try a new cuisine at a locally owned restaurant

Fun is everywhere if we stay curious.

Joy as Resistance

Here's something radical: In a world that profits from your exhaustion, your joy is an act of resistance. In a culture that tells you your worth is tied to your productivity, choosing delight is a revolutionary act.

Your joy declares:
- You are more than what you produce.
- You deserve good things simply because you exist.
- God's goodness extends beyond your usefulness.
- Life is meant to be lived, not just survived.

Empowerment Truth: When you model joy, you give others permission to experience it too.

Applying the GRACE Method:

☐ **G: Ground Yourself in God's Truth:** God created joy and delights in your delight. Let that sink in.

☐ **R: Reflect on Your Current Reality:** Are you experiencing enough joy?

☐ **A: Act with Intentional Steps:** Choose one joyful activity to do this week.

☐ **C: Create Consistent Systems:** Schedule weekly joy moments, just as you would a meeting.

☐ **E: Embrace Progress Over Perfection:** Joy doesn't have to be extravagant; it just has to be real.

Reflection Questions:

1. When was the last time you truly had fun?
2. What did you do?
3. What are three joyful activities you can plan for this month?

4. What's one joy blocker you need to release?
5. How can you invite more fun and play into your family or friendship circles?

Prayer for Joy:

Heavenly Father,

Thank You for creating joy and delight. Forgive me for the times I believed I wasn't worthy of fun or rest. Help me to see joy as a gift, not a luxury. Fill my heart with laughter again. Open my eyes to the small delights You place in my path each day. Let my life be marked not only by responsibility, but by rejoicing. Teach me how to rest, laugh, dance, and live with the complete freedom of Your love.

In Jesus' name, Amen.

Your time to dance is now.

THE JOY-FILLED WOMAN'S BUCKET LIST: BECAUSE FUN IS HOLY, TOO

Why a Bucket List Matters

A bucket list isn't just about thrill-seeking or checking off exotic destinations. *It's a declaration that you matter.* That your dreams, your laughter, your wild ideas, deserve space in your real life.

It's about saying yes to adventure, creativity, beauty, and even the silly stuff. When life gets heavy or predictable, this list becomes a light. A reminder that you're not just here to serve and survive, you're here to live.

This is your invitation to rediscover who you are beyond your roles, titles, and responsibilities. Let's create a life full of memories, joy, and soulful experiences on purpose.

The Ultimate Bucket List for Women (25–55): Simple Everyday Joys

☐ Try a new recipe from a different country.
☐ Buy yourself fresh flowers just because.
☐ Watch the sunrise and write down your thoughts and feelings.

- ☐ Read an entire novel in a weekend.
- ☐ Host a themed dinner night at home.
- ☐ Visit a local farmers' market and cook what you find.
- ☐ Take a nap in the middle of the day (guilt-free!)
- ☐ Send a handwritten letter to someone you love
- ☐ Take a 24-hour social media detox and do something playful in stead.
- ☐ Have a solo picnic with your favorite snacks and book.

Playful + Fun Activities

- ☐ Take a dance class (hip hop, salsa, line dancing, etc.)
- ☐ Go to a silent disco or karaoke night.
- ☐ Try roller skating or ice skating again, even if you're rusty!
- ☐ Book a makeover session just for fun.
- ☐ Dress up for no reason and do a photo shoot.
- ☐ Watch an uplifting comedy and laugh out loud.
- ☐ Host a paint-and-sip night with girlfriends.
- ☐ Take a hula hoop or jump rope challenge.
- ☐ Ride a bike through a scenic trail.
- ☐ Learn a trending TikTok dance with your kids (or on your own!)

Creative + Soulful Expression

- ☐ Take a pottery, watercolor, or photography class.
- ☐ Start a gratitude or prayer journal.
- ☐ Decorate a space in your home that reflects you.
- ☐ Write a short story or poem just for fun.
- ☐ Make a vision board and hang it where you can see it daily.
- ☐ Start a book club with a few women you admire and respect.
- ☐ Record a voice note to your future self.
- ☐ Try adult coloring books or mandalas for a mindful activity.
- ☐ Learn to play an instrument (even basic guitar or piano)
- ☐ Join a local choir or music group.

Leisure + Nature Experiences

☐ Visit a botanical garden or arboretum.
☐ Go berry picking or apple picking in season.
☐ Take a sunrise or sunset hike.
☐ Kayak or paddleboard at a local lake.
☐ Try zip-lining or a ropes course.
☐ Go glamping or try an Airbnb treehouse.
☐ Visit a waterfall and take in the sound.
☐ Take a long scenic drive with your favorite playlist.
☐ Do a "no phone" nature walk, just you and God.
☐ Stargaze from your backyard or a nearby park.

Travel + New Adventures

☐ Travel solo (even if just a day trip!)
☐ Plan a girls' weekend getaway.
☐ Take a train ride to a city you've never explored.
☐ Visit a place you've always dreamed of as a child.
☐ See a Broadway-style show in your nearest major city.
☐ Stay in a beach house or a mountain cabin.
☐ Tour a historic site or cultural museum.
☐ Book a spa weekend or self-care retreat.
☐ Do an ancestry trip to explore your heritage.
☐ Try a food tour in a nearby town.

Community + Connection

☐ Volunteer for a cause you're passionate about
☐ Take someone on a "surprise joy date."
☐ Organize a neighborhood potluck or game night.
☐ Mentor a younger woman or teen girl.
☐ Host a "Come As You Are" brunch.
☐ Start a women's prayer or encouragement circle.
☐ Plan a legacy video and record messages for your loved ones.
☐ Support a local business or pop-up shop.
☐ Attend a women's empowerment or faith-based event.
☐ Create a family memory jar and fill it weekly.

BUCKET LIST PLANNING WORKSHEET

Step 1: Name Your List: Give your bucket list a title that reflects your season or spirit (e.g., "Joy in My 30s" or "My Year of YES")

Step 2: Circle 10 You Want to Try This Year: Start with just 10 things that spark something in your spirit. Don't overthink it. Circle what excites you.

Step 3: Pick 3 to Do This Month: From your 10, pick *three activities* to complete this month. Schedule them on your calendar like appointments with joy.

Journal Prompts for Living Fully

1. What would I try if I weren't worried about failing or looking silly?
2. What does "fun" look like for the woman I'm becoming?
3. Which activities restore my joy, laughter, or peace the most?
4. What's one memory I want to make this year, and with whom?
5. What would it look like to live more fully, one bold step at a time?

Final Empowerment Truth

You were not created to merely manage life. You were created to live it, fully, joyfully, and abundantly. So go ahead, make the memory, say yes to the moment, try the wild idea, and let your life reflect the joy and glory of the God who created you.

CHAPTER 20

Giving: You're Blessed to Be a Blessing

The Sacred Art of Giving and Receiving

It is more blessed to give than to receive. — *Acts 20:35, NIV*

The Giving Trap That's Stealing Your Joy:

Let me ask you something tender but real: how many times have you poured out for others today (your energy, your emotional bandwidth, your kindness) and felt drained instead of fulfilled? As women, we are often applauded for how much we give. But somewhere along the way, we started associating giving with sacrifice only, instead of sacred overflow.

We give rides, meals, advice, hugs, prayers, favors, and patience. And still, we carry the quiet question in our hearts: Is it okay to stop giving? Is it okay to rest? The truth? You were never meant to give from a state of depletion. God calls us to a life of generosity, but never at the cost of our well-being. This chapter is your permission slip and your invitation to return to joyful, intentional, God-powered generosity.

The Joyful Generosity God Intended

God's kind of generosity isn't about guilt or exhaustion. It's about partnering with heaven. It's a posture of open hands and open hearts, trusting that the same God who pours into us will pour through us. Generosity is not limited to your bank account. It's in how you show up:

- With your time
- With your attention
- With your words

- With your prayers
- With your gifts and talents
- With your testimony

Whether you are in a season of financial abundance or just making ends meet, you already have something to give. That something may be your wisdom, your listening ear, your laughter, or simply your presence. It all matters, so much more than you know.

Start With the Right Mindset

Generosity begins in the heart. Ask yourself: Am I giving from fear or faith? From guilt or grace? When you believe that God is your Source, you don't fear running out. You trust that every seed you sow, every word, every dollar, every gesture, is planted into soil that will bear fruit in due season.

Give, and it will be given to you. They will pour into your lap a good measure— pressed down, shaken together, and running over {with no space left for more}. For with the standard of measurement you use {when you do good to others}, it will be measured to you in return. — Luke 6:38, AMP

Coaching Insight: Generosity is not about how much you have; it's about how open your heart is to share it. Even a kind word can be a divine assignment.

Give From Right Where You Are

You don't always need a surplus to have an impact. The smallest, most sincere gifts are often the most powerful.

Here are simple ways to give right now:

- Text a word of encouragement.
- Pay for someone's coffee or toll.
- Deliver dinner to a new mom.
- Babysit for a single parent.
- Send a voice note praying over someone's dreams.
- Donate items you no longer use.
- Speak life to a discouraged friend.

- Offer to pray, right then and there.

You will be enriched in every way so that you may be generous, and this {generosity, administered} through us is producing thanksgiving to God {from those who benefit}. — 2 Corinthians 9:11, AMP

Daily Affirmation: *"I don't need to wait for more. I can give from what I already have."*

Use What's Already In Your Hands

Ask yourself: What do I already have that could be a blessing to someone else? Are you a great organizer, a fabulous cook, a nurturing spirit, or someone who always knows the right words? God has uniquely gifted you. He didn't bless you for you to hide it; He blessed you to multiply it through love and service.

Each of you should use whatever gift you have received to serve others...
— 1 Peter 4:10, NIV

Real Life Reminder: In our journey as a family of nine, there were many seasons where money was tight, but I always had time, wisdom, or encouragement to offer. That still made a difference. And your offering does too.

Turn Your Pain Into Purpose: When Scars Become Seeds

Some of the most beautiful acts of generosity don't come from our strengths; they come from our experiences that required healing. The scars we carry are not signs of weakness; they are testimonies of survival. They speak of nights we thought would break us, and the mornings we chose to rise anyway. When surrendered to God, our pain becomes the soil in which purpose grows.

That divorce you never saw coming. That miscarriage that still makes you tear up in grocery store aisles. That season of loneliness when you felt invisible in your own home. That betrayal that shattered your trust in people, and maybe even in God. That health scare that turned your world upside down. That prodigal child who still hasn't come home. None of it was wasted.

You see, you are the answered prayer someone is waiting for. Not because your life is perfect now, but because you're still standing, still believing. Still choosing hope when giving up would be easier. You survived to give the lessons, the encouragement, the advice, the comfort, or the listening ear to those who come behind you in that life experience.

He comforts us in all our troubles so that we can comfort others.
— *2 Corinthians 1:4, NLT*

God never wastes your pain. He repurposes it into power, empathy, and ministry. And remember..."Weeping may endure for a night, But joy comes in the morning" (Psalm 30:5, NKJV). Share your journey back to joy with someone.

Real-Life Empowerment:

Maybe your healing journey is still in process. That's okay. Even in the middle of your mess, God can use you. Sometimes your *"I understand"* is the most healing phrase another woman will hear all week.

Coaching Prompt: From Wound to Witness

Take a moment and reflect.

1. What is one painful experience that shaped who you are today? It might still ache. That's okay. It means there's depth and purpose there.

2. What strength did God build in you through it? Maybe it's compassion, patience, wisdom, or fierce resilience.

3. Who could your story serve? It might be a friend, a sister, a co-worker, or even a stranger in line at the grocery store. You don't need a microphone or a ministry title. You just need a willing heart.

Write it down. Pray over it. Then ask God to show you who needs to hear it, and when He does, trust that your scar is someone else's roadmap to healing.

Legacy Over Lack: The Scarcity Trap

When we live from fear, saying things like "I don't have enough time, money, energy," we parent from fear, we serve from fear, and we love from fear. But when we live from abundance, we teach others how to live free.

You are not called to hoard, hustle, and hope for scraps. You are called to flow, give, and build generational blessing.

The generous will themselves be blessed, for they share their food with the poor.
— *Proverbs 22:9, NIV*

Practical Legacy Action Steps:

1. Model Generosity in Front of Your Children or Mentees

- Let them see you tithe, give, and bless others without strings attached.
- Let them help pick gifts for a family in need or drop off meals to someone grieving.
- Invite them into the why: "We do this because God has been good to us."

2. Start a Legacy Journal

- Write down your values, stories of faith, and lessons learned in hard times.
- Create blessing letters for your children, mentees, or spiritual daughters. Leave something to read long after you're gone.

3. Host a Legacy Dinner

- Gather your family or friends. Share stories of ancestors, faith moments, and declarations of who you are becoming.
- Speak over your children the identity and blessings you want them to carry.

4. Establish a Monthly Giving Ritual

- Choose a day of the month when you give intentionally, whether it's

money, time, or encouragement.
- Teach those around you that generosity isn't a special occasion; it's a lifestyle.

Empowerment Truth:

You may never see the full impact of your legacy, but heaven will. Every act of obedience, every seed of kindness, every intentional choice to live generously ripples into eternity.

You are not too late to start. You are not too small to matter. You are not too stretched to give meaningfully. Your legacy is not what you leave in your will; it's what you live with your will every day.

Let Your Giving Reflect What You Value

Where your money, time, and energy go reveals what your heart values. Are you supporting the causes that matter to you? Are you investing and sowing in your local church, helping widows, single mothers, youth programs, or missions? What causes do you care about the most?

Where your treasure is, there your heart will be also. — Matthew 6:21, NIV

Reflection Prompt:
Does where I give align with what I truly care about?

Build Habits of Daily Generosity

Make generosity a rhythm, not a random act. Start small. Let it become second nature.

Practical Habits:
- Begin each day with: "Lord, show me whom to bless today."
- Keep a "generosity jar" in your home for spontaneous giving.
- Include giving in your monthly budget.
- Involve your kids or mentees in blessing someone weekly.

This isn't about pressure; it's about purpose.

Let Go of Fear and Hoarding: Open Hands, Open Heart

Have you ever felt like you were clenching your fists just to make it through the week, holding on tightly to your time, your money, your energy, your boundaries? Fear will do that. Fear tells you:

- "If I give too much, there won't be anything left for me."
- "If I serve again, I'll be taken advantage of."
- "If I spend this now, I won't have it when I really need it."

But here's the truth: Hoarding is rooted in fear, not faith. And the more we hoard our resources, our talents, our time, the less room we create for divine multiplication. God doesn't bless clenched fists. He blesses open hands.

One person gives freely, yet gains even more; another withholds unduly, but comes to poverty. — Proverbs 11:24, NIV

This isn't just about money. This is about mindset. It's about the posture of your heart when you give, serve, show up, or release what no longer serves you.

Coach Truth: What you release in faith, God multiplies. What you cling to in fear begins to shrink. That dream you're afraid to pursue because it might "fail"? That money you're afraid to invest in yourself or your healing? That "yes" you're holding back because you're afraid it'll cost too much? What if the real cost is not moving in obedience?

Coaching Reflection: What Are You Holding Too Tightly?

Take a breath and ask yourself:

1. What resource am I clinging to out of fear (money, time, energy, space, affection)?
2. What belief is driving that fear? (e.g., "There won't be enough," "No one will support me," "If I give, I'll go empty.")
3. What might God be asking me to release, so He can refill me?

Releasing is Not Recklessness. It's Trust.

Letting go doesn't mean living without wisdom. It means trusting God enough to follow His rhythm. He is a God of both sowing and reaping: feasting and fasting, pouring out and being filled. And here's the kingdom paradox: When you release in faith (your time, your money, your emotional labor), you make room for divine overflow. The loaves and fish multiplied when they were placed in Jesus' hands, not when the disciples kept them "just in case." The limits can be broken off of your life when you follow God's plan for doing and being. Start giving, ask God to bless it, and see what happens.

Empowerment Tip: Practice Small Releases Daily

You don't need a grand act of generosity to break free from fear. You just need a faithful act.

- Give a compliment even when you feel unnoticed.
- Spend $10 to bless someone else when you're worried about your own budget.
- Say "yes" to that divine nudge, even if you're unsure how it'll all work out.

That's not losing control. That's choosing trust.

Create a Vision for Kingdom Impact

Ask yourself: If I had more than enough, how would I use it to bless others? Don't wait until you "arrive." Start now on your current level. God blesses movement, not perfection.

Journal Prompt: If I had more than enough, I would give to ____. This week, I will take a small step by ____.

You Are Already a Blessing

You don't need a title, platform, or perfect life to be generous. You just need a willing spirit. You have been blessed to be a blessing. Your story, your hugs, your wisdom, your tears, your time, they all carry power. And when you give them with intention, you change lives.

I am convinced and confident of this very thing, that He who has begun a good work in you will {continue to} perfect and complete it until the day of Christ Jesus {the time of His return}. — Philippians 1:6, AMP.

Applying the GRACE Method

☐ **G: Ground Yourself in God's Truth:** Remember that God is your Source and Sustainer. Your generosity doesn't deplete you; it positions you.

☐ **R: Reflect on Your Current Reality:** Are you giving from overflow or obligation? Is your giving life-giving or soul-draining?

☐ **A: Act with Intentional Steps:** Choose one generous act today aligned with your strengths or gifts. Keep it simple, but meaningful.

☐ **C: Create Consistent Systems:** Add generosity to your calendar, budget, or family rhythm. Make it a habit, not a one-time thing.

☐ **E: Embrace Progress Over Perfection:** Start where you are. Don't wait until you feel like "enough" to bless others. You are already enough.

Reflection Questions

1. How has your definition of generosity changed after reading this chapter?
2. In what ways have you been giving from depletion rather than overflow?
3. What small gifts or experiences from your life could be turned into blessings for others?
4. How can you start incorporating your family or children into a lifestyle of generosity?
5. What would it look like for your generosity to reflect your core values?

A Prayer for the Generous Heart

Father,

Thank You for being the ultimate Giver. You gave us life, love, grace, and purpose. Help me to reflect Your heart in how I give, not from guilt, not for applause, but from joy, trust, and love. Show me where I'm holding back out of fear.

Teach me to give from overflow and discern the assignments that are truly mine. Make me a woman of open hands and an open heart. Let my life be a river of blessing, flowing from You and into the lives of those around me. Multiply every seed I sow, and let my generosity become a legacy of love.

In Jesus' name, Amen.

CHAPTER 21
Making It a Lifestyle

Becoming Whole: Living Loved and On Purpose Every Day

Let us not grow weary in doing good, for at the proper time we will reap a harvest if we do not give up. — Galatians 6:9, NIV

Some people call it a lifestyle. I call it becoming whole. This chapter isn't about going back to the old version of you. It's about stepping into the most aligned, grace-filled, and powerful version of who God created you to be. The one who walks in peace, not just for a season, but for a lifetime. The one who no longer waits for external validation but lives in rhythm with God's love and divine purpose.

You weren't created just to survive the hard seasons. You were created to live loved, lead with courage, and thrive in every area: spiritually, emotionally, relationally, physically, and financially.

And here's the truth: You don't need a complete life overhaul every few months. What you need are sustainable rhythms, rooted in grace, built with intention, and nourished by the Spirit.

So, how do you actually live this way, especially when life gets busy, when routines unravel, and when you're tempted to go back to old habits? You build a lifestyle of wholeness with four key anchors.

Four Key Anchors:

1. Stack Habits with Purpose

You've already planted powerful seeds throughout this journey: new ways of thinking, fresh commitments, better routines and rhythms. Now it's time to water those seeds daily with intention. Because transformation doesn't just happen in the big moments; it's sustained in the small, quiet, repeated, consistent ones.

Habit stacking is one of the most grace-filled, effective ways to build sustainable change. It simply means attaching a new habit to something you already do consistently, such as making coffee, brushing your teeth, or going to bed. This technique removes the mental burden of "starting from scratch" and helps your new routine or rhythm become automatic.

Biblical Backing: "So whether you eat or drink or whatever you do, do it all for the glory of God." (1 Corinthians 10:31, NIV). That means every moment, no matter how ordinary, is an opportunity to honor God and nourish your soul.

Here's how it looks:

- After I make my coffee, I read one scripture aloud and thank God for something simple.
- While brushing my teeth, I say a morning affirmation: "I am loved. I am chosen. I am equipped for today."
- Before I check my phone, I take three slow, grateful breaths and ask: "God, what would You have me focus on today?"
- When I fold laundry, I pray over each person whose clothing I touch.
- When I press start on the dishwasher, I speak a blessing over my home: "Peace lives here."

These aren't just chores; they become sacred touchpoints. Little blessed, consecrated habits. Small hinges that open big doors.

Empowerment Tip: Your habits don't have to be complicated. They simply need to be consistent, intentional, and aligned with your values. This isn't about perfection. It's about creating rhythms that pull you toward peace, not pressure.

Habit Stack Builder Prompt

Use this simple phrase to start creating your own stack:

After I [current habit], I will [new habit]

Example: After I pour my water in the morning, I will declare one promise of God over my day.

Coach Truth: You don't need a long routine. You need a meaningful one: one that aligns your heart, not just your calendar.

Start with one or two. Let them anchor your day. And watch how these small daily decisions begin to rewire your mindset, reset your spirit, and rebuild your life one gentle step and stack at a time.

2. Build Support: Accountability with Heart

Growth isn't meant to be lonely. Healing isn't meant to happen in isolation. And the journey toward purpose and peace was never designed to be a solo mission. If the enemy can isolate you, he can discourage you. But when the right voices surround you, the ones who speak life, truth, and courage, you become unstoppable.

Accountability isn't about pressure. It's about partnership. It's about having someone in your life who knows where you're going, believes in what God is doing in you, and gently nudges you forward when you're tempted to shrink back. Think of it as treasured, divinely ordered sisterhood.

Invite someone into your journey, not because you're weak, but because you're wise. Whether it's a close friend, a trusted mentor, a prayer partner, or even a new sister from your women's group, God will often place people in your life to walk beside you. Don't be afraid to open that door.

Here's how to make it practical and powerful:

Schedule Weekly Check-Ins: Whether it's a quick Sunday text, a Wednesday coffee date, or a shared journal via email, having a regular rhythm of checking in creates structure, and it reminds you that you're not doing this alone.

Share Honestly: Let them know what you're working on. Be vulnerable about the setbacks, not just the successes. Accountability rooted in grace, not guilt, is the soil where real transformation grows.

Celebrate Small Wins: Did you say no to a toxic pattern? Did you choose rest instead of rushing? Did you stick to your morning prayer habit three days in a row? That's worth celebrating. These are the building blocks of breakthrough.

Scripture Anchor

Two are better than one... If either of them falls down, one can help the other up.
— *Ecclesiastes 4:9–10, NIV*

This is your reminder that God never intended for you to rise alone. Sometimes the miracle isn't just in your progress; it's in your people.

Coach Prompt: What if your obedience became someone else's inspiration? What if your yes gave someone else the courage to believe again? Your consistency could unlock someone else's breakthrough. Don't underestimate the power of being seen, known, and cheered on.

3. Reflect Quarterly: Don't Just Set Goals, Review Them

So many of us race through life with our heads down, checking off boxes, pouring into others, and pushing through exhaustion, without pausing to ask: Is this even working?

Reflection isn't a luxury. It's a lifeline. And you don't have to wait for New Year's Eve to evaluate where you are. What if, every 90 days, you created a silent, sacred space to breathe, assess, and realign your life with your God-given purpose? This isn't about perfection, it's about presence. It's about turning down the noise of comparison and tuning in to what matters most.

Use a Grace-Filled Quarterly Life Review:

Ask yourself:

- What's going well? Celebrate wins, no matter how small. Progress is holy.
- Where am I feeling drained or misaligned?
- Look at your routines, relationships, and responsibilities. Are they fueling your growth, or exhausting your soul?
- What do I need to surrender or simplify? Sometimes pruning is necessary for purpose to flourish.
- What is God speaking over this next season of my life? Take time to

journal, pray, and listen. God's voice often whispers through reflection.

Coach Insight: Realignment is not failure, it's wisdom. Give yourself permission to adjust your goals based on new revelations, shifts in season, or updated priorities. You are allowed to pivot.

Legacy Reminder: The most impactful women aren't necessarily the busiest; they're the most aligned. They move with clarity. They say no with confidence. And they build lives that reflect heaven's rhythm, not hustle culture.

> *Teach us to number our days, that we may gain a heart of wisdom.*
> — *Psalm 90:12, NIV*

4. When You Lose Momentum: Return to Grace

You're not going to get it right every single day, and that's not a prediction of failure; that's a promise of your humanity. Life will life. Kids will get sick, deadlines will pile up, emotions will surprise you, and sometimes the routines you've worked so hard to build will fall through the cracks.

That doesn't make you a failure; it makes you a woman who is living. A woman who is learning. A woman who is still deeply loved in the middle of the mess.

The real danger isn't in dropping the ball. It's in the voice that whispers, "You'll never get it back." The lie that says one off day, one off week, or one backslide somehow erases all the progress you've made. But here's what God says instead:

Though the righteous fall seven times, they rise again. — *Proverbs 24:16, NIV*

Not *if* you fall. *When.* Because even the righteous, even the ones chasing purpose and doing the work, fall. But we rise again. With love. With grace. With divine resilience.

So if you haven't opened your journal in a week? No shame, just start again today.

If your wellness plan fell apart after that vacation or emotional week?

Deep breath, lace up again. If your boundaries got blurry or your mindset turned negative? You're still growing, refocus again.

What you don't have to do is punish yourself to prove you're still worthy. You don't have to restart from scratch, hustle to make up for lost time, or drown in guilt.

The most powerful thing you can do is return to grace. Grace that welcomes you home without shame. Grace that says, *"Let's begin again, right here."*

Coach Truth: Wholeness was never about perfection. It's about persistence. It's about showing up again and again from a place of love, not pressure.

You are allowed to start over. You are allowed to evolve. You are allowed to be a work in progress and a masterpiece simultaneously. Give yourself grace, and then get back in the game, wiser and more anchored than ever.

Living Loved Isn't a Luxury. It's a Lifestyle.

Living loved is not a reward for doing everything right. It's not reserved for the days when the to-do list is finished, the work projects are all completed, the kids are quiet, and the house is spotless. It's your birthright as a daughter of God. You were created in love, rescued by love, and are sustained by love, daily.

You don't have to hustle for wholeness. You don't need to earn peace. You don't have to chase validation, applause, or perfection. The love you're looking for isn't "out there" in someone's approval or your next accomplishment. It's already yours. Right now. In Christ.

So whether today feels productive or peaceful, messy or miraculous, show up for your life with love. Show up for your dreams with grace. And show up for your family with intention.

Let your routines be rooted in love, not performance. Let your rest be sacred, not something you feel guilty for. Let your presence, not your perfection, be your greatest offering.

You're not going back to who you were. That version of you was surviving. This version of you is rising, healing, creating, and becoming. You're becoming the woman God always knew you'd be: whole, joyful, purposeful, and deeply, undeniably loved.

Applying the GRACE Method

☐ **G: Ground Yourself in God's Truth:** Revisit one scripture each morning that reminds you of who you are in Christ.

☐ **R: Reflect on Your Current Reality:** What's helping you thrive? What needs adjusting?

☐ **A: Act with Intentional Steps:** Choose one habit to build with purpose this week.

☐ **C: Create Consistent Systems:** Implement a morning or evening reset routine.

☐ **E: Embrace Progress Over Perfection:** Celebrate showing up, even imperfectly.

Reflection Questions

1. What new habit can I stack onto something I already do daily?
2. Who can I invite into my growth journey for encouragement and accountability?
3. What does "living loved" look like for me in this season?
4. How can I make room for grace when I fall short?

Prayer for Wholeness and Alignment

Father,

Thank You for walking me through every page of this journey. I'm not the same woman I was when I began, and I praise You for that. Help me carry this healing, wisdom, and joy into my everyday life. When I forget, remind me. When I fall, lift me. When I doubt, surround me with Your truth. Let my lifestyle reflect Your love. Let my days be marked by grace. Teach me to live loved, on purpose, and in alignment with heaven's call.

In Jesus' name, Amen.

ACCOUNTABILITY PARTNER AGREEMENT WORKSHEET

Purpose: To walk in partnership with grace, encouragement, and mutual support as we grow into the women God is calling us to be.

Accountability Partner Names:
Partner A: _____
Partner B: _____

Our Shared Commitment Statement:

We commit to showing up for each other with honesty, compassion, consistency, and prayer. We will celebrate progress, extend grace in the face of setbacks, and hold each other accountable to our highest purpose, not perfection.

We Agree To:

Frequency of Check-Ins:

- ☐ Daily
- ☐ Weekly
- ☐ Biweekly
- ☐ Monthly

(Choose one and write day/time if applicable)

_____

Preferred Method of Communication:

- ☐ Text
- ☐ Phone Call
- ☐ Video Chat
- ☐ In Person
- ☐ Shared Journal or Google Doc

Confidentiality Agreement: Everything shared between us remains confidential. We commit to creating a safe and non-judgmental space for growth and truth.

Encouragement Promise: We agree to remind each other that progress matters more than perfection. We will speak life, not shame, into one another's journey.

Partner Goals:

My top 1–2 goals this season:

1. _____

2. _____

How I want to be supported:

☐ Accountability check-ins
☐ Encouragement on hard days
☐ Help breaking down big goals
☐ Prayer support
☐ Gentle reminders
☐ Other: _____

Signature & Date:

Partner A: _____ Date: _____

Partner B: _____ Date: _____

WEEKLY CHECK-IN TEMPLATE

Date: _____

1. One Win From This Week:

2. What am I proud of or celebrating?

3. One Challenge I Faced:

4. What felt hard, frustrating, or draining?

5. What Helped Me Stay On Track:

6. What system, mindset, scripture, or habit supported me?

7. One Thing I Want to Improve Next Week:

8. Where do I want to shift or show up more intentionally?

This Week I Will...

- ☐ Set one small goal
- ☐ Focus on a healthy habit
- ☐ Choose joy on purpose
- ☐ Reach out to my partner

Specific Intentions:

Prayer Request or Scripture Anchor for the Week:

Accountability Partner Notes:

Checklist:
- ☐ Encouraged my partner
- ☐ Checked in
- ☐ Shared my updates

90-DAY LIFE REVIEW TEMPLATE & JOURNAL WORKSHEET

Reflect, Realign, and Refresh Your Life Every 90 Days

1. Gratitude Reflection

- What were three highlights or blessings from this past quarter?

- Where did I see God's faithfulness show up in unexpected ways?

2. Spiritual Health Check-In

- How is my prayer life and connection with God right now?

- What spiritual practices have helped me grow?

- What do I feel God is inviting me into in this next season?

3. Emotional & Mental Health Check-In

- How have I been managing stress, rest, and joy?

- What situations or relationships have drained me?

- What has brought me peace and energy?

4. Physical Health & Wellness Check-In

- How have I taken care of my body this quarter?

- What routines have helped me feel strong and whole?

- Where do I need more grace or more discipline?

5. Relationships & Community

- Who have I been pouring into?

- Who has poured into me?

- Are there any boundaries I need to set or strengthen?

- Who do I want to reconnect with or invest more time in?

6. Purpose & Productivity

- What goals did I move forward this quarter?

- What projects or dreams need to be reprioritized?

- Where have I been overcommitted or underaligned?

7. 90-Day Reset Prompts

- What is one habit I want to grow in this next quarter?

- What's one thing I will release to make room for peace?

- What would success feel like in the next 90 days?

- What is my word or scripture for the upcoming quarter?

My 90-Day Declaration:

"In this next season, I will show up with intentionality, grace, and trust. I will honor my growth, release what no longer serves, and stay aligned with what God is calling me to."

RETURN TO GRACE: JOURNAL PROMPTS

Use these prompts whenever you feel off track, overwhelmed, or in need of a gentle reset.

1. Where do I feel like I've fallen behind, and what emotion is attached to that feeling? (Shame, guilt, fear, frustration? Name it without judgment.)
2. What story am I telling myself about this setback? Is it true?
3. What does God say instead?
4. What grace do I need to offer myself today?
5. What do I need to hear most from my own heart?
6. What small, life-giving action can I take today to realign with peace and purpose?
7. What am I proud of myself for, even in this imperfect moment?

RETURN TO GRACE: RESET CHECKLIST

This gentle checklist is for the days when you feel scattered, defeated, or "off." It's not about checking every box; it's about returning to what grounds you.

☐ I spoke to myself kindly today.
☐ I paused and took three deep, centering breaths.
☐ I prayed or reflected, even briefly.
☐ I moved my body with love or stretched with intention.
☐ I drank water and nourished myself with something wholesome.
☐ I reached out to someone safe or uplifting.
☐ I forgave myself for yesterday's mess.
☐ I named one thing I'm grateful for today.
☐ I reminded myself: Progress, not perfection, grace, not guilt.

Coach Reminder: You don't need a flawless routine to be a faithful woman. You just need a heart that keeps returning to God, to your vision, and to grace.

90-Day Roadmap

Conclusion: The Journey Continues

You Were Born for This Moment

Now to Him who is able to {carry out His purpose and} do superabundantly more than all that we dare ask or think {infinitely beyond our greatest prayers, hopes, or dreams}, according to His power that is at work within us.
— Ephesians 3:20, AMP

Beautiful friend...Before you turn the page or rush back into the whirlwind of life, I want you to pause, breathe, and let this truth settle in your spirit: **You did it. You made it.**

You didn't just read a book; you took a brave, decisive step toward your transformation. You chose to show up for yourself in a season where most people would have just kept surviving. You journaled. You prayed. You reflected. You let truth sink into the cracks where burnout and self-doubt once lived. You allowed healing, vision, and restoration to enter.

And that tells me everything I need to know about you: you're not just hoping for change, you're committed to it. This journey wasn't a checklist. It was a calling. And you answered it with your whole, beautiful heart.

The Woman Who Began This Journey Is Not the One Finishing It

Maybe when you began these pages, you were running on fumes. Perhaps you felt invisible, disconnected, discouraged, or like you were pouring from an empty cup every single day.

You may have been smiling on the outside, but secretly wondering if anyone saw the weight you were carrying. But today? You've become a woman who knows her worth. A woman who is rooted in grace, who walks with intention, who sees rest as sacred and joy as holy. You've traded hustle for healing. Survival for strategy. Shame for strength. And the best part? You're just getting started.

What You've Built Is Bigger Than a Goal

These 90 days weren't about becoming a new woman; they were about becoming the real you. The one God already sees. The one you may have forgotten under all the pressure, performance, and people-pleasing.

You've:

☑ Reconnected with your divine identity
☑ Rebuilt habits around grace and purpose
☑ Reclaimed your voice, your rhythm, and your peace
☑ Realigned your life with what truly matters
☑ Remembered that wholeness isn't something you earn; it's something you embrace.

And now that you've laid the foundation, you can build something that lasts, not just for you, but for every woman watching you rise.

You Are the Ripple

Whether you realize it or not, your courage is contagious. When you reclaim your joy, you teach your children it's safe to be whole. When you honor your calling, you give your friends permission to dream again. When you live from grace, you lead with peace instead of pressure.

Your life becomes a living, breathing testimony of what's possible through faith and purpose. So don't underestimate what you just did because a woman living in alignment with her calling becomes a lighthouse for generations.

What Happens When the Glow Fades?

This high won't last forever. Life will test your routines and rhythms. You'll forget your affirmations. You'll skip your journaling. Guilt or fear may sneak back in. But here's the truth: A setback is not the end. A detour is not disqualification.

Wholeness isn't about being perfect. It's about returning to grace again and again. So when you stumble, return to your GRACE Method. When you feel lost, return to God's promises. When you feel alone, return to this community. And always return to the truth: You are still the woman for the job.

Your Legacy Begins Now

You weren't just made to get through life. You were made to live it fully with joy, faith, and fire. What you do today, how you love, serve, rest, and rise, ripples far beyond what you can see.

As you step into this next season, remember: You were chosen for such a time as this. Your story still matters. Your best days are not behind you; they're being written right now. And I'll be right here, cheering you on the whole way.

Ready to Keep Growing?

Let's keep walking together. Because this isn't goodbye; it's your launch. Join the empowered Mom Life with Marla Community. It's where sisterhood meets strategy, where we laugh, cry, pray, and grow together.

Inside you'll find:

- Weekly encouragement and check-ins
- Individual coaching
- Group coaching and Q&A sessions
- Faith-fueled articles, journal prompts, and templates
- A sacred space with women who get it

Join us at momlifewithmarla.com - We're saving a seat for you.

Need More Support? Book a 1:1 Coaching Session

If you need clarity, courage, or just someone to remind you of who you are, let's talk. I offer custom empowerment sessions rooted in prayer and practical wisdom to help you walk boldly into your next chapter. Schedule at momlifewithmarla.com.

Spread the Movement

If this book changed you, share it. Gift it. Post about it. Leave a review. There's another woman out there just like you, tired, hopeful, ready, and she's waiting for this message. On social media, use #CreateTheLifeYou-WantNow and help us grow this global sisterhood.

A Final Word From My Heart

I didn't write this as an expert. I wrote this as a sister. As a mom who has cried in the bathroom and as a woman who has had life situations that hit me so hard I felt as if I could not catch my breath, let alone take the next step. I wrote this as a woman who lost herself multiple times, and found her way back through the grace of God.

You are not behind. You are not too late. You are not too much. You are enough. You are deeply loved. And you were born for this moment.

The thief comes only in order to steal and kill and destroy. I came that they may have and enjoy life, and have it in abundance {to the full, till it overflows}.
—John 10:10, AMP

Let that be your truth. Let that be your guide. Take the next step toward abundance and creating the life you want, now. Let that be your legacy.

With every ounce of love and belief in you,
— Marla
Your Empowerment Coach, Your Sister in Purpose,
And Your Witness to the Wonder You're Becoming

A Prayer of Salvation

If you've never asked Jesus into your heart, or if you've drifted and you're ready to come back home. I want to personally invite you to pray this simple but life-changing prayer with me.

You don't have to have all the answers. You don't need to be perfect or have it all together. Just come with an open heart. God loves you deeply, and He's been waiting for this moment.

It would be my greatest joy to walk with you into the most important relationship you will ever have. Take a breath. Open your heart. Let's pray.

Heavenly Father,

Thank You for loving me, even when I didn't realize how much I needed You. Today, I acknowledge that I've tried to do life on my own, and I've fallen short. But I believe that You sent Your Son, Jesus, to die for my sins and rise again so that I could be forgiven, healed, and made whole.

Jesus, I invite You into my heart right now. Be my Lord, my Savior, and my forever friend.

Wash me clean. Make me new. Help me to live the life You created me for, full of purpose, joy, peace, and truth.

I surrender my past, my pain, my plans, and my pride. From this day forward, I choose to follow You. Lead, grow, and surround me with people who will walk this faith journey with me.

Thank You for saving me. Thank You for loving me. And thank You for never giving up on me.

In Jesus' name I pray, Amen.

Supporting Scriptures:

If you declare with your mouth, 'Jesus is Lord,' and believe in your heart that God raised him from the dead, you will be saved.
—*Romans 10:9 (NIV)*

For God so loved the world that he gave his one and only Son, that whoever believes in him shall not perish but have eternal life. —*John 3:16 (NIV)*

Anyone who belongs to Christ has become a new person. The old life is gone; a new life has begun! — *2 Corinthians 5:17 (NLT)*

For it is by grace you have been saved, through faith—and this is not from yourselves, it is the gift of God. —*Ephesians* 2:8 *(NIV)*

If you just prayed that prayer, welcome home, beautiful friend. Heaven is rejoicing, and so am I! You are fully known, fully loved, and finally found. Keep going. Keep growing. You are never alone again.

ABOUT THE AUTHOR

Marla A. McCarthy is an empowerment life coach, speaker, and founder of Mom Life with Marla, a global movement that equips women, especially moms, to stop merely surviving and start living with intention, purpose, and joy.

With degrees in Exercise Science Education from The Ohio State University and Healthcare Administration, Marla combines academic insight with real-life and faith-based coaching. She holds multiple certifications, including Master Life Coach, Empowerment and Self-Care Coach, Goal Success Coach, Transformation Life Coach, and more, equipping her to guide women through all seasons of life.

But her deepest wisdom was forged not in a classroom, but in the trenches of motherhood, marriage, and personal healing. As a mother of seven children, Marla knows what it's like to feel invisible while being desperately needed, to pour out endlessly, and wonder if your dreams still matter. Her journey from burnout to breakthrough birthed a calling: to help women rediscover their voice, reclaim their peace, and rise into the life they were created to live.

Through her coaching, books, online programs, and faith-based resources, Marla teaches women how to build lives that reflect both faith and ambition, service and self-care, family and purpose. Her clients affectionately call her a "truth-teller wrapped in grace", someone who loves you enough to meet you where you are, but won't let you stay stuck.

Today, Marla coaches women worldwide, speaks at retreats and women's conferences, leads empowerment group coaching communities, and still manages her most sacred role, being a present, purpose-driven wife and mom to her six sons and daughter. Her signature message is simple but life-changing:

You don't have to choose between being a good woman and being a fulfilled woman. You were created to be both.

Connect with Marla

Visit MomLifeWithMarla.com to join the movement, book a coaching session, or explore her latest books and courses. Follow on Instagram: @momlifewithmarla. For speaking, coaching, or media inquiries, contact her team at momlifewithmarla.com.

Topical Scripture Index

About Prayer:
Deuteronomy 28:13
I Chronicles 4:10
Nehemiah 8:10b
Psalm 23:4
Psalm 37:4
Isaiah 53:5
Isaiah 54:17
Matthew 6:9-13
Mark 1:35
Mark 9:29
Mark 11:22-23
Luke 6:38
John 14:14
Romans 8:31
Philippians 4:13
II Timothy 1:7
Hebrews 11:1
I John 1:9
I John 4:4
1 John 5:14-15

Anger:
Psalm 37:8-9
Proverbs 14:16-17
Proverbs 14:29
Proverbs 15:1
Proverbs 16:32
Proverbs 25:21-22
Ecclesiastes 7:9
Matthew 5:22-24
Matthew 6:14
Romans 12:19
Ephesians 4:26
Ephesians 4:31-32
Colossians 3:8
Hebrews 10:30
James 1:19-20

Answered Prayer:
Psalm 37:4
Psalm 91:15
Psalm 145:18-19
Proverbs 15:29
Isaiah 65:24
Jeremiah 33:3
Matthew 6:6
Matthew 7:7-8
Matthew 18:19-20
Matthew 21:22
Mark 11:24
John 14:13
John 15:7
John 16:23
Hebrews 4:16
I John 3:22

Being a husband:
Proverbs 12:4
Proverbs 12:15
Proverbs 18:22
Proverbs 19:14
Proverbs 31:11
Proverbs 31:23
Proverbs 31:28
Ecclesiastes 9:9
Mark 10:12
Luke 16:18
Romans 7:2
1 Corinthians 7:2
1 Corinthians 7:3
1 Corinthians 7:4
1 Corinthians 7:9-11
1 Corinthians 7:14-16
Ephesians 5:23
Ephesians 5:25

Ephesians 5:33
Colossians 3:19
I Timothy 3:2
I Timothy 3:12
Titus 1:6
1 Peter 3:7

Being a wife:
Psalm 128:3
Proverbs 5:18-19
Proverbs 12:4
Proverbs 12:15
Proverbs 14:1
Proverbs 18:22
Proverbs 19:14
Proverbs 31:11
Proverbs 31:10-31
I Corinthians 7:3
Ephesians 5:21-33
Colossians 3:18
I Peter 3:1-7

Career & Business:
Deuteronomy 8:18
Deuteronomy 28:1-6, 8, 11-13
Joshua 1:8
I Kings 2:2-3
I Chronicles 22:13
Job 36:11
Psalm 1:1-3
Psalm 127:1
Proverbs 3:5-10
Proverbs 16:3
Proverbs 24:3-4
Isaiah 48:17
Matthew 6:33
Romans 12:11
Colossians 4:1
I Thessalonians

Matthew 5:31-32
Matthew 19:3-9
Mark 10:2-12
Luke 16:18
I Corinthians 7:10-
    17

Doubt:
Psalm 18:30
Isaiah 46:10-11
Isaiah 55:10-11
Isaiah 59:1
Mark 11:22-24
Luke 12:29-31
Romans 4:20-21
Romans 10:17
I Thessalonians 5:24
I Peter 4:12-13
II Peter 3:9

Effective Prayer:
Isaiah 1:15-16
Zechariah 7:8-13
Matthew 6:6
Matthew 14:23
Mark 1:35
2 Corinthians 7:14-
    15
Ephesians 1:15-19
Colossians 4:2, 12
1 Thessalonians
    5:17
James 5:16

Faith:
Matthew 9:20-22
Matthew 9:28-29
Matthew 17:20
Mark 9:23

Mark 11:22-24
Romans 1:17
Romans 10:17
Romans 12:3
II Corinthians 5:7
Hebrews 11:1
Hebrews 11:6
Hebrews 12:2
James 5:14-15
I Peter 1:7-9
I John 5:4

Family:
Exodus 20:12
Deuteronomy 6:6-9
Joshua 24:15
Psalm 127:3-5
Psalm 128:1-4
Proverbs 13:22
Proverbs 17:6
Proverbs 22:6
Proverbs 23:24
Proverbs 29:17
Isaiah 54:13
Malachi 4:6
Acts 16:31
Ephesians 4:31-32
Ephesians 5:21-6:4
Ephesians 6:4
I Timothy 3:4-5

Fear:
Psalm 23:4-5
Psalm 27:1, 3
Psalm 31:24
Psalm 56:11
Psalm 91:1
Psalm 91:4-7
Psalm 91:10-11

Proverbs 3:25-26
Isaiah 54:14
John 14:27
Romans 8:15
Romans 8:29, 31,
    35-39
II Timothy 1:7
Hebrews 13:5-6
I John 4:18

**Financial
Problems:**
Deuteronomy 8:7-
    14, 18
Deuteronomy 28:2-
    8
Deuteronomy
    28:11-13
Joshua 1:8
Psalm 23:1
Psalm 34:10
Psalm 37:25
Proverbs 13:22
Ecclesiastes 2:26
Malachi 3:10-12
Matthew 6:31-33
Matthew 10:8
Matthew 19:29
Luke 6:38
I Corinthians 16:2
II Corinthians 9:6-8
Philippians 4:19
III John 1:2
Forgiveness:
Isaiah 43:18-19
Matthew 5:10-12
Matthew 5:44
Matthew 6:14-15
Matthew 18:21-22

Mark 11:25
Luke 17:3
Romans 12:21
Ephesians 4:31-32
Philippians 3:13-14
Colossians 3:13
Hebrews 10:30
I Peter 2:19-23
I Peter 3:9-10
I Peter 4:12-14

God's faithfulness:
Genesis 9:16
Genesis 28:15
Deuteronomy 7:8-9
Joshua 23:14
I Kings 8:56
Psalm 36:5
Psalm 40:10
Psalm 89:1
Psalm 89:2
Psalm 89:5
Psalm 89:8
Psalm 89:33-34
Psalm 92:2
Psalm 119:65
Psalm 119:90
Psalm 121:3-4
Psalm 143:1
Isaiah 25:1
Isaiah 54:9-10
Lamentations 3:23
1 Corinthians 1:9
I Corinthians 10:13
I Thessalonians 5:24
II Thessalonians 3:3
II Timothy 2:13, 19
Hebrews 10:23
I Peter 4:19

II Peter 3:9
I John 1:9

God's Guidance:
Joshua 1:8
Psalm 16:11
Psalm 18:30
Psalm 19:7
Psalm 19:9-11
Psalm 23:3
Psalm 32:8
Psalm 37:23
Psalm 119:9-11
Psalm 119:24
Psalm 119:105
Proverbs 6:22-23
Proverbs 16:25
Isaiah 2:3
Isaiah 30:21
Luke 1: 70, 79
John 8:31-32
John 10:3
II Timothy 3:16-17
II Peter 1:4

God's Will:
Exodus 33:13
Joshua 1:8
Nehemiah 9:20
Psalm 17:5
Psalm 25:4-5
Psalm 31:3
Psalm 32:8
Psalm 37:23-24
Psalm 43:3
Psalm 48:14
Psalm 119:105
Psalm 119:133
Psalm 143:8

Psalm 143:10
Proverbs 3:5-6
Proverbs 6:22-23
Proverbs 16:3
Isaiah 30:21
Isaiah 48:17
Isaiah 58:11
John 16:13
James 1:5

Grief:
Psalm 23:4
Psalm 119:50
Isaiah 41:10
Isaiah 43:2
Isaiah 49:13
Isaiah 51:11
Isaiah 61:1-3
Jeremiah 33:3
Matthew 5:4
I Corinthians 15:55-57
II Corinthians 1:3-4
II Corinthians 5:8
I Thessalonians 4:13-14
II Thessalonians 2:16-17
Hebrews 4:15-16
I Peter 5:7
Revelation 21:4

Health & Healing:
Exodus 15:26
Psalm 103:3
Psalm 107:20
Proverbs 4:20-22
Isaiah 53:5
Jeremiah 17:14

Jeremiah 30:17
Matthew 8:8
Matthew 9:35
Mark 16:17-18
Luke 6:19
John 6:63
Hebrews 13:8
James 5:14-15
I Peter 2:24
III John 1:2

Joy:
Nehemiah 8:10
Psalm 16:11
Psalm 30:5
Psalm 105:43
Psalm 126:5
Ecclesiastes 2:26
Isaiah 51:11
Habakkuk 3:18
John 15:10-12
John 16:20
John 16:24
Acts 2:28
Romans 5:11
Romans 14:17
Romans 15:13
Galatians 5:22
Philippians 4:4
Jude 1:24

Loneliness:
Deuteronomy 4:31
Deuteronomy 31:6
Deuteronomy 33:27
I Samuel 12:22
Psalm 27:10
Psalm 46:1
Psalm 147:3

Isaiah 41:10
Isaiah 54:10
Matthew 28:20
John 14:1
John 14:18
Romans 8:35-39
Hebrews 13:5
I Peter 5:7

Love:
Jeremiah 31:3
Mark 12:30-31, 33
John 3:16
John 13:34-35
John 14:21
John 15:9-10
John 15:12-14, 17
John 16:27
Romans 5:8
Romans 8:38-39
I Corinthians 13:1-
   8, 13
I John 4:7-8
I John 4:10-12
I John 4:16, 21

Marriage:
Genesis 2:18
Genesis 2:24
Proverbs 3:5-6
Proverbs 18:22
Jeremiah 29:6
Hosea 2:19, 20
I Corinthians 7:2-4
Ephesians 5:22-33
I Timothy 5:14
Hebrews 13:4
I Peter 3:1
I Peter 3:7

Marital Problems:
Genesis 2:18
Genesis 2:24
Joshua 24:15
Psalm 101:2
Psalm 119:1-2
Proverbs 3:5-6
Proverbs 10:12
Romans 13:10
Ephesians 4:31-32
Ephesians 5:21-33
I Peter 1:22
I Peter 3:1-7
I Peter 3:8-11

Patience:
Psalm 27:14
Psalm 37:7
Psalm 37:8-9
Psalm 40:1
Ecclesiastes 7:8-9
Isaiah 40:31
Lamentations 3:26
Romans 5:3-5
Romans 8:25
Romans 15:4-5
Galatians 5:22
Hebrews 6:12
Hebrews 10:35-37
Hebrews 12:1
James 1:3-4
James 5:7-8

Peace:
Psalm 37:11
Psalm 37:37
Psalm 119:165
Proverbs 17:14

Isaiah 26:3
Isaiah 26:12
Isaiah 55:12
Isaiah 57:2
John 14:27
Romans 5:1
Romans 8:6
Romans 12:18
Romans 14:17-19
Romans 15:13
II Corinthians 13:11
Philippians 4:6-7
Colossians 3:15
James 3:16

Pleasing God:
II Chronicles 5:13, 14
Psalm 47:1
Psalm 109:30
Psalm 145:21
Psalm 147:11
Psalm 149:1-6
Isaiah 43:7, 21
John 4:23, 24
Romans 8:8-9
Romans 12:1-2
Colossians 1:10
I Timothy 2: 1, 3, 8
Hebrews 11:6
Hebrews 13: 15-16
I Peter 2:5, 9
I John 3:22
Revelation 4:11

Prayer for Others:
Deuteronomy 9:26
1 Samuel 1:27
1 Kings 8:48-50
2 Chronicles 7:14

Ezra 6:10
Nehemiah 1:11
II Corinthians 13:14
Philippians 1:9-11
Colossians 1:9-11
I Thessalonians 5:23
II Thessalonians 2:16-17
II Thessalonians 3:5
Hebrews 13:20-21

Prosperity:
Deuteronomy 8:18
Deuteronomy 26:1-2
Deuteronomy 28:2
Joshua 1:7
Psalm 35:27
Psalm 112:1, 3
Proverbs 1:32
Proverbs 3:9-10
Proverbs 13:21
Proverbs 22:7
Malachi 3:10-12
Luke 6:38
2 Corinthians 9:7-8
Galatians 3:29
Galatians 6:7
Ephesians 4:28
Philippians 4:19
I Timothy 6:17
III John 1:2

Protection:
Psalm 91

Salvation:
Matthew 10:32
John 1:12

John 3:16
John 3:17
John 3:36
Romans 3:23
Romans 5:8
Romans 5:12
Romans 6:23
Romans 10:8-10
1 Corinthians 15:1-4
Ephesians 2:8-9
I John 5:11-13
Revelation 3:20

Single Life:
Psalm 37:4
Proverbs 3:5-6
Proverbs 12:15
Hosea 2:19
Romans 7:4
1 Corinthians 6:13
1 Corinthians 6:18
I Corinthians 7:8-9
I Corinthians 7:27-28
I Corinthians 7: 32-33, 35
I Corinthians 7:37
Galatians 6:4
Hebrews 13:4
II Peter 1:6-8

Spiritual Growth:
Psalm 92:12
II Corinthians 3:18
Ephesians 3:14-19
Ephesians 4:14-15
Philippians 1:6, 9-10

Colossians 1:9-11
Colossians 3:16
I Timothy 4:15
II Timothy 2:15
Hebrews 6:1
I Peter 2:2-3
II Peter 1:5-8
II Peter 3:18

Temptation:
Psalm 119:11
Proverbs 28:13
Romans 6:14
I Corinthians 10:12-13
Ephesians 6:10-11, 16
Hebrews 2:18
Hebrews 4:14-16
James 1:2-3, 12
James 1:13-14
James 4:7
I Peter 1:6-7
I Peter 5:8-9
II Peter 2:9
I John 1:9
I John 4:4
Jude 24-25

Trials & Troubles:
Psalm 31:7
Psalm 121:1-2
Psalm 138:7
Isaiah 43:2
Isaiah 51:11
Nahum 1:7
Matthew 6:34
John 14:1
John 16:33

Romans 8:28
II Corinthians 1:3-4
II Corinthians 4:8-9
Philippians 4:6-7
Hebrews 4:15-16
I Peter 5:7

Unsatisfied:
Psalm 34:10
Psalm 37:3
Psalm 63:1-5
Psalm 103:1-5
Psalm 107:9
Proverbs 12:14
Isaiah 1:19
Isaiah 12:2-3
Isaiah 44:3
Isaiah 55:1
Jeremiah 31:14
Joel 2:26
Matthew 5:6
Matthew 6:33
II Corinthians 9:8
Philippians 4:12-13

Unsaved Loved Ones:
Genesis 22:18
Psalm 55:22
Psalm 98:2
Proverbs 22:6
Isaiah 44:3
Isaiah 50:10
Isaiah 56:1
Matthew 18:14
John 16:7-8
Acts 11:14
Acts 16:31
I Corinthians 7:13-16

I Thessalonians 5:21-22
I Thessalonians 5:24
I Peter 3:1-2
II Peter 3:9

Victory:
Psalm 33:10
Isaiah 1:19
Isaiah 54:17
Matthew 7:7
Mark 11:24
John 1:4-5
John 16:33
Romans 8:37
I Corinthians 15:57
II Corinthians 2:14
II Corinthians 4:17
Ephesians 6:13-17
Philippians 4:13
I Thessalonians 5:18
II Timothy 2:3
I Peter 5:9-10
I John 2:14
I John 4:4
I John 5:4
I John 5:5

Waiting:
Psalm 27:14
Psalm 33:20
Psalm 62:5
Psalm 130:5
Psalm 145:15-16
Isaiah 25:9
Isaiah 40:31
Habakkuk 2:3
Hebrews 10:23

Hebrews 3:14

Widows:
Deuteronomy 10:18
Deuteronomy 27:19
Job 29:13
Psalm 68:5
Psalms 146:9
Psalm 147:3
Proverbs 15:25
Isaiah 54:5
Jeremiah 49:11
Matthew 28:20
John 14:18
John 16:22
I Corinthians 7:39-
    40
Philippians 4:19
Hebrews 13:15
James 1:27

Wisdom:
Job 12:13
Proverbs 1:7
Proverbs 2:6-7
Proverbs 3:13
Proverbs 4:7-9
Proverbs 5:1
Proverbs 8:11
I Corinthians 3:19
James 1:5, 3:16-18

Worry:
Psalm 4:8
Psalm 91:1-2
Psalm 119:165
Proverbs 3:24
Isaiah 26:3
Matthew 6:25-34

John 14:1
John 14:27
Romans 8:6
II Corinthians 2:14
Philippians 4:6-7
Philippians 4:19
Colossians 3:15
Hebrews 4:3, 9
I Peter 5:6-7

ALSO AVAILABLE FROM

THE REAL LIFE SERIES PUBLISHING CO.

Create The Life You Want:
90-Day Goal Journal
by Marla A. McCarthy
ASIN: B0F4W9YRP7
Available at Amazon.com

Enhancing Your Journey:
90-Day Prayer Journal
by Marla A. McCarthy
ASIN: B0F37TRD72
Available at Amazon.com

Enhancing Your Journey:
A Biblical Guide To A More Powerful Prayer Life
by Marla A. McCarthy
ISBN: 979-8-9989754-3-1

The Ten Commandments of Friendship:
Sisterhood Principles Every Woman Should Live By
by Marla A. McCarthy
ISBN: 979-8-9989754-4-8

Loving Me:
A Guide To Renewing Your Mind, Body & Spirit
by Marla A. McCarthy
ISBN: 979-8-9989754-5-5

Be a Seed:
Grow Deep. Rise Strong. Multiply Good
by Marla A. McCarthy
ISBN: 979-8-9989754-6-2

www.ingramcontent.com/pod-product-compliance
Lightning Source LLC
Chambersburg PA
CBHW021712120626
46545CB00004B/1526